PRAISE FOR *GEOSTRATEGY BY DESIGN*

"There has never been a more important time for enterprises to build a geostrategic capability, and this book explains how to do that. The authors draw upon their own cutting-edge research, which shows how this era of dramatic global change requires the rapid and purposeful development of a new organizational muscle—the ability to make decisions that align the organization with the changing global landscape. Those who follow the path laid out by this book, and specifically its geostrategy framework for strategic political risk management, will be the winners in the current and future world."

—Nick Lovegrove, Professor of the Practice, McDonough School of Business, Georgetown University; Senior Partner Emeritus, McKinsey & Company

"*Geostrategy by Design* comes at a critical time. The current geopolitical environment is forcing CEOs to adapt their operations, strategies, and governance structures. This book provides a long-overdue and indispensable guide for what executives can actually do to manage the geopolitical risks they face."

—Janet Truncale, EY Global Chair and CEO

"The definitive corporate geostrategy how-to guide. Timely, compelling, and a must-read for business leaders braving the uncharted geopolitical waters of the next decade."

—Cameron Mitchell,
Head of Geopolitical Risk, ANZ Banking Group

"Take advantage of today's complex global environment. *Geostrategy by Design* is a must-read for any executive seeking to not only survive but thrive in today's complex world. The authors outline concepts and relationships which are applicable to any organization—without being overly prescriptive. Applied correctly, businesses will become more resilient and even better identify opportunities that otherwise would have been completely unknown."

—**Jill Sanborn**, FBI Senior Executive for National Security (Retired) and former Senior Director of Geopolitical Strategy, Roku

"Today is a time of many simultaneous crises, all of which have potential repercussions on business. How do executives cope with the many challenges? Ignoring them is no option. Neither is following one's gut feeling. A systematic approach is needed. This is exactly what this book is about. In a very convincing way, employing practical examples, the authors design a comprehensive strategy which will allow executives to successfully navigate through these challenging times. A must read!"

—**Ambassador Christoph Heusgen,** Chairman of the Munich Security Conference

"Rising volatility and more uncertainty has led to sleepless nights for business executives operating in the global business environment today. *Geostrategy by Design* is essential reading for those seeking to better anticipate, plan, and mitigate the geopolitical risks that threaten enterprises. The book offers a practical framework to aid companies in the essential analysis of geopolitical risks and mitigation strategies, illustrated with relevant real-world examples. Every company needs a geostrategy."

—**Carolyn Brehm**, retired Vice President for Global Government Relations and Public Policy, The Procter & Gamble Company

"In a world where political risk is omnipresent, business executives need to pay close attention to the wider world. Executives need to 'scan' the horizon and stay attuned not only to direct risks but also to second and third-order challenges. *Geostrategy by Design* offers a framework to enable businesses to tackle political risk. Clear examples combined with practical advice will allow C-suite executives to better navigate an increasingly complex business world."

—**Steven Fox,** Executive Chairman, Veracity Worldwide

"*Geostrategy by Design* makes a compelling case that C-suites and boards must now recognize the importance of geopolitical change, move away from the ad hoc and reactive responses, and bring greater structure to considering the consequences of geopolitical change for their companies. In setting out the steps that can help firms do this, the book provides business readers with a critical practical contribution to the emerging debate on how best this can be done."

—**Derek Leatherdale,** Managing Director, GRI Strategies Ltd.

"Books on political risk tend to be either academic and impractical or shallow and lacking informed context on organizational dynamics. This book brilliantly charts a path forward with rigor and clarity, and explains how executives today can consider and integrate an increasingly chaotic and dynamic external risk landscape. The book benefits greatly from the combination of deep practical experience with rigorous research and compelling case studies, and ought to be required reading for all executives running global businesses in the 2020s."

—**Alison Taylor,** Clinical Associate Professor, NYU Stern
School of Business; author of *Higher Ground: How Business
Can Do the Right Thing in a Turbulent World*

"*Geostrategy by Design* is the go-to strategy navigator through the geopolitical storms on the horizon. Much has been written on change management in business, but what will truly create top quintile performers is a proactive strategy to embrace the fundamental uncertainty on the horizon."

—**Terence Lyons,** CEO, The Stakeholder Company

"After a period of globalization, geopolitical risk and global conflict are top of the list for global companies. This thoughtful and well researched book will be an invaluable resource for senior leaders everywhere."

—**Daniel Diermeier,** Chancellor of Vanderbilt University; author of *Reputation Rules: Strategies for Building Your Company's Most Valuable Asset* and *Reputation Analytics: Public Opinion for Companies*

GEOSTRATEGY

BY

DESIGN

GEOSTRATEGY

BY

DESIGN

HOW TO MANAGE GEOPOLITICAL RISK
IN THE NEW ERA OF GLOBALIZATION

COURTNEY RICKERT McCAFFREY,
WITOLD J. HENISZ, AND OLIVER JONES

DISRUPTION
BOOKS
New York, NY • Washington, DC

Published by Disruption Books
New York, New York
www.disruptionbooks.com

Distributed by Disruption Books

For information about speaking engagements or business inquiries, please contact EY at strategyandtransactions@ey.com. For information about special discounts for bulk purchases, please contact Disruption Books at info@disruptionbooks.com.

Cover and book design by *the*BookDesigners

Library of Congress Cataloging-in-Publication Data available

Print ISBN: 978-1-63331-073-5
eBook ISBN: 978-1-63331-074-2

First Edition

*To my fellow political scientists and corporate
strategists, in the hope that you can collaborate more
in the future, and to my family for their support
(Courtney Rickert McCaffrey)*

*To the geostrategists who inspire me with their journey,
my students who aspire to follow them,
and Marcia, Sophie, and Katya for making
our own journey (Witold J. Henisz)*

*To all those who work to make our world a safer place,
and to William, Georgina, and Eloise, who I hope
get to live in a safer world (Oliver Jones)*

CONTENTS

INTRODUCTION

How do executives position a company for growth when the geopolitical future is uncertain? At this moment of deep and broad geopolitical transition—during a pivot when one era of globalization is being replaced by another—executives are being forced to ask themselves that question. That's where "geostrategy" comes into play—namely the holistic and cross-functional integration of political risk management into broader risk management, strategy, and governance. Previous generations of corporate executives have faced similar dilemmas, having to overcome challenges and seize opportunities associated with political risks, albeit in different contexts. Despite the uniqueness of the current geopolitical environment, those previous eras of volatility can point the way toward growth and prosperity in the new era of globalization.

History can teach us a great deal. In the late 1980s, as the Cold War drew to a close, analysts argued about what might come next. Some professed an optimistic zeal, confident that, with the reduced threat of nuclear apocalypse, the world would become more economically and politically integrated. Businesses once boxed out (or hemmed in) by the Iron Curtain would now be able to access new markets and establish new supply chains. A nation rich in natural resources would now be able to supply a new diversity of markets. Another country's prestigious universities could draw students from around the globe. A company with the best technology could serve customers globally. The possibilities seemed endlessly enticing.

But another school of thought was less optimistic. Skeptics saw danger in what amounted to a prospective global crack-up. Economies that had long depended on Soviet subsidies now appeared poised to devolve into social unrest. Old, repressed resentments might suddenly come to the fore. In 1992, a Harvard professor named Samuel P. Huntington delivered a lecture that would eventually form the basis of a best-selling book titled *The Clash of Civilizations and the Remaking of World Order*, arguing that cultural cleavages were destined to dominate the future. For all the promises offered by visions of a post–Cold War world, this school of thought suggested that any new global order was likely to continue to be characterized by conflict—but that conflict would be between civilizations rather than countries.

That uncertainty put the world's business leaders in an uncomfortable position. Even amid the specter of menace, the Cold War had provided the private sector with a degree of certainty and predictability. Now, amid a shifting global architecture, many companies' fates depended on predicting that future. Was it wise to lean into the change, or better instead to wait until the realities of the globe's new post–Cold War geopolitical architecture began to come into starker relief? These were crucial geostrategic decisions.

The global automobile industry offers one compelling example of how geostrategic decisions had a material impact on companies. By the late 1980s, Toyota had already established itself as one of Japan's leading automakers. But in many other major markets around the world, the company played more on the margins. Toyota's car production in the large European market, for example, only accounted for about 3 percent of its total overseas production.[1] And in the US, Toyota competed only in the market for small sedans—with their Camrys and Corollas—and executives were eager to begin serving consumers looking to purchase luxury cars, sport utility vehicles, and pickup trucks.[2]

It was only as the post–Cold War era of globalization dawned that company executives were faced with making big geostrategic decisions—and Toyota decided to lean into the change. In the early 1990s, new "Guiding Principles" at Toyota were formulated. It was reported that Toyota "President Shoichiro Toyoda indicated that he did not want something that was 'in keeping with the times,' but rather a set of principles that would 'lead the times.' As such, those responsible embarked on establishing a course that would help Toyota become a truly international corporation."[3]

Toyota's leadership used geostrategic thinking to plot the way forward, refusing to be dissuaded by the fear of change. The company began selling its luxury automobiles, vans, SUVs, and trucks to American consumers who, up to that point, had depended on other manufacturers. But the company's geostrategic expansion didn't end there.

Executives also began investing elsewhere—not so aggressively that the company was at such grave risk that it would not survive some regional and international tension. But the Japanese manufacturer began making careful investments in Southeast Asia, Latin America, and Eastern Europe such that the company would be able to scale up quickly in the event that a truly global market emerged.

Today, of course, we know how things turned out. During the three decades that followed the Berlin Wall's collapse, the global economy did become more integrated. Market barriers fell, just-in-time manufacturing flourished, and efficiency became a lodestone of success. And Toyota's geostrategic bet paid off. From 1990 to 2000, Toyota's annual overseas production of vehicles more than doubled.[4] And the share of Toyota's vehicle sales in foreign markets rose from 50 percent in 1990 to 66 percent in 2000.[5]

Toyota is and was, of course, an enormous enterprise, and its successes and failures hinge on factors beyond executives' approaches to geopolitical change. But part of the story is that Toyota, having used geostrategic thinking to take advantage of changing geopolitical circumstances that led to a wave of globalization, thrived in the decades that followed in large part because it leaned into the change. And it's that clear lesson that executives need to appreciate today: amid ongoing geopolitical uncertainty, C-suites and boards who wait for clarity run the risk of being elbowed aside by aggressive first movers who may corner scarce resources or market positions that followers struggle to replicate. For that reason, executives need to act expeditiously, even when presented with imperfect or incomplete intelligence, to make strategic decisions that position their companies to flourish in the next era of globalization.

That doesn't mean companies should be haphazard—Toyota, in fact, was very strategic about its various investments, hedging risks carefully so it would be able to pivot if new barriers emerged to global commerce. But as we'll argue in the pages that follow, the company's willingness to lean into change in the early, uncertain days was a key to its success in the decades that followed. And that's what executives need to keep in mind today.

Now, for the first time since the end of the Cold War, the architecture of the global economy is shifting dramatically. The outlines of the new era of globalization are only just beginning to emerge, but will be defined by shifts in the system of global alliances and the degree to which governments continue to engage in statist economic policies. What is clear already is that the contours, risks, opportunities, and rhythms of commerce are being fundamentally upended. And that means corporate executives now must face a set of geostrategic concerns that simply weren't present just a few years ago. They have to develop a better understanding of how the world is poised to evolve—how geopolitical, national, regulatory, and societal concerns are likely to impact their businesses down the road. They have to begin preparing their companies for a level of geostrategic uncertainty that did not exist during the last three decades.

This book was written as a practical guide to tackling those dilemmas—an increasingly urgent, strategic imperative in this rare, uncertain moment. In the course of any given individual career of, say, 40 years, major geostrategic shifts present themselves once or perhaps twice. They tend to define the bounds of success for several subsequent decades. So, if you are fortunate enough to be leading a company at a moment of dramatic, global, political change, you can't afford *not* to take advantage. And so, that's what this book was designed to do—to help you understand how to design and implement a geostrategy for your company to be ready to take advantage of the shifts inherent in the new era of globalization.

THE POST-COLD WAR WORLD

A lot has changed since the Berlin Wall's collapse more than three decades ago. New technologies have emerged. Certain sectors have emerged; others have been rendered obsolete. But the broader geopolitical dynamics that emerged at the end of the Cold War have largely remained stable. And it's worth noting, as we enter the next era of globalization, what has defined the world as it was, if only so we can begin to appreciate just how dramatically the crucial pillars of the world we inherited are now giving way to a new global architecture.

First, during this era of heady globalization, capitalism came to prevail as the de facto economic model. It did not prevail everywhere, and it had its fair share of crises. But for three decades, markets, rather than states, served as the primary drivers of global economic conditions, with varying degrees of regulation depending on circumstance. And multilateral institutions were given the authority, in most cases, to set the rules of the game.

Second, for the bulk of the last three decades, the business world was able to take for granted a relatively free flow of international trade between points all around the globe. For that reason, business success largely hinged on keeping pace with the efficiency born from exploiting competitive advantages—harvesting more affordable raw materials in one place, nurturing pockets of deep capabilities in another, and serving markets hungry for specific products or services in a third. Global reach became the norm.

Third, the global middle class grew at leaps and bounds, drumming up new demand for middle-class goods and services year over year. That shift, in turn, fueled a wave of new global consumption, establishing new markets around the world, many of which are now being served by a growing network of global megacompanies born from a combination of mergers, acquisitions, and technological advancements.

Finally, the post–Cold War era was defined by the world's shift from analog to digital. That shift has forced businesses to reimagine their products and services, and required them to create a whole new realm of marketable items. That interconnectivity has morphed from being a luxury to now being more of a "given" for many households and businesses around the world.

This suite of post–Cold War "givens" shaped corporate decision-making for three decades. Successful executives built corporate strategies based on the presumption that these four pillars would serve as the foundation for future growth. To that end, up until recently, a company could reasonably pursue a strategy targeting expansion in nearly every corner of the globe, assuming the proposal made proper economic sense.

It was that set of presumptions that gave executives license to put such a heavy premium on "efficiency." In a world with low levels of geopolitical risk, executives felt compelled to pursue linear global supply chains, to seek out less costly labor markets, and to build complex relationships with various vendors. And in a world with very few limitations on cross-border capital flows, executives pursued M&A and other direct investments in markets around the world, regardless of their political systems and geopolitical alliances. And while some paid close attention to environmental, social, and governance (ESG) concerns, most shareholders focused on revenues and profits, paying closer attention to measures of efficiency.

THE RE-EMERGENCE OF GEOSTRATEGIC IMPERATIVES

More recently, however, the post–Cold War era has given way to a new chapter in the emerging history of globalization. It's not that businesses aren't still focused on profitability, growth, and efficiency. It's not that the global interconnectedness is poised for a wholesale reversal. But, in ways that would have been virtually unfathomable not so long ago, the pillars that girded the recent era of globalization have begun to shift. Those shifts require not just slight adjustments, but a fundamentally different way of thinking. If companies are going to thrive in the next era of globalization, their drive for efficiency must be balanced with their ability to anticipate not only commercial, but also geopolitical change, and to adapt to newfound perpetual churn and high levels of uncertainty.

Some have come to believe that globalization has ended—that the period bookended by the fall of the Berlin Wall and, say, the onset of the war in Ukraine was an aberration, almost as though the economy is now set to revert to some historical reality. But the evidence simply doesn't support that overly simplistic view. Globalization isn't *ending*—it's evolving. And while it's certainly possible that national economies could become more monolithically insular in the decades to come, that's hardly the most likely scenario. Any sober analysis makes it clear that the globe is likely to stay deeply connected in the future, but those connections will evolve amid a much more complicated and dynamic set of national and international relationships. The *next* era of globalization will be built on a different set of pillars.

To understand the forces that will shape globalization in the decades to come, we have to acknowledge the cracks in the foundation of the pillars that supported the heady globalization in the last three. First, a series of crises, ranging from the global financial crisis between 2007 and 2009 to the COVID-19 pandemic, shook global faith in capitalism. As a result, the orthodox view that political considerations should yield to the wisdom of financial markets—a key element of what's known as the "Washington Consensus"—was significantly challenged. The global financial crisis that began in 2007 gave credence to what is now a more widespread belief that social dynamics, climate change, and other considerations deserve more weight when balanced against the demands of free markets.

Second, populism and nationalism have re-emerged with a vengeance after decades on the wane. That perhaps was clearest with Brexit, a remarkable break within a European bloc that seemed otherwise poised to become more, rather than less, integrated. But examples abound across the world. The rise of the "Make America Great Again" movement in the US is another salient example. And nationalism is on display in more specific aspects of life and business today as well: the emergence of digital nationalism and "vaccine nationalism" during the height of the COVID-19 pandemic are just two such examples. What's becoming clear is that the old notion prevalent during the previous era of globalization, that "place doesn't matter," has been rendered obsolete. People may not be retreating from the globalized economy entirely, but populations remain rooted in senses of identity that are, once again, emerging as important geopolitical vectors.

Third, social- and class-oriented fissures are becoming more pronounced across the globe. Economists, such as Thomas Piketty, have demonstrated that inequality within many countries became *more* pronounced during the post–Cold War era of globalization.[6] But overall economic growth papered over these issues for a time. Nevertheless, various feelings of grievance have remained potent within and between some communities. By some measure, flagging faith in capitalism and a renewed attention to the distribution of income and wealth gave space for old rivalries to re-emerge: urban vs. rural, the working class vs. the middle class, and one tribe vs. another. And they have. In his book, *The Crisis of Democratic Capitalism*, Martin Wolf argues the simultaneous crises of confidence in democracy and confidence in capitalism are intertwined in important ways— with the lack of widely shared prosperity resulting in these social fissures that threaten democracy.[7]

Fourth, primarily as a result of the first three changes, the trading blocs that emerged during the post–Cold War era have begun to devolve. The World Trade Organization, for example, no longer sits quite so squarely at the center of global commerce. In its place, other more regional groups are beginning to play more powerful roles. For example, the Regional Comprehensive Economic Partnership (RCEP) established a new set of ties between Australia, China, Japan, New Zealand, South Korea, and the 10 members of the Association of Southeast Asian Nations (ASEAN). And, importantly, the new trading relationships and broader patterns of economic flows are increasingly driven by geopolitical alliances and the presence of common political ideologies, rather than by primarily economic considerations.[8]

Finally, while digitization has become virtually ubiquitous in societies around the globe, the connectivity revolution it augured has more recently begun to take an unexpected turn. Digital barriers between economies—"data localization" as some term it—have become more common, and certain technologies have more recently been made subject to export controls. Information can now be manipulated and even weaponized as "fake news" or worse. And rapid technological change is supercharging this situation. For all the promise of artificial intelligence (AI), and generative AI (GenAI) in particular, these technologies risk exacerbating such social challenges. So, while many once presumed that technological advances would serve to bridge the chasms that often emerge between peoples, it's now clear that digitization and related, emerging technologies can cut the other way as well.

Those five trends, when combined, suggest that the contours of globalization's next era will be very different in both spirit and reality from what came before. Supply chains and markets of all sorts will be increasingly fractious. A decade ago, C-suite executives could reasonably expect that component parts sourced around the world would be *more* accessible—that trade barriers were poised to fall—but that's no longer realistic. If they believed that most national populations would remain reasonably stable or that international institutions would remain the mortar of an interdependent world or that long-term bilateral alliances would hold true, they now need to keep a more open mind about how the future may evolve.

WHAT WE KNOW ABOUT TOMORROW

Recent events have accelerated a shift toward a multipolar world. It is currently defined by three emerging spheres or blocs. Developed markets are leading one bloc, with the EU and US having reached new levels of cooperation. Russia is at the center of a second small bloc of countries, including several autocracies. Finally, a significant number of emerging markets—including, most notably, India—are not fully aligned with either of these blocs, preferring to pursue a more neutral, multi-aligned or transactional stance—at least for now. And China's geopolitical positioning remains more complex, straddling the latter two camps. But there is no guarantee that this trajectory will continue. We don't know exactly how these blocs will evolve—but that's the essential point. Whereas the alliances that defined the last 30 years were fairly stable and also fairly inconsequential in terms of their effects on companies' strategies, the environment today has become much more dynamic and material. And that's why geostrategy is becoming a more important centerpiece of corporate thinking.

The impacts of this new global architecture will differ from industry to industry and company to company. But businesses, in particular, that operate in an evolving set of strategically important sectors—including semiconductors, telecommunications equipment, electric vehicles (EVs), pharmaceuticals, and critical infrastructure—are likely, in coming years, to be subject to new government interventions. In some cases, that may spur supply chain disruptions. In others, it will impact market access. In others, government will likely take a stronger hand in determining the permissibility of cross-border investment, including M&A. And, in still others, businesses are likely to face more regulatory scrutiny, including stricter antitrust standards.

But it's not just firms in these strategically important sectors who will face complications as the globe's architecture changes. If a company's research is developed within one of these blocs, but its products are manufactured in another, it is likely to be much more vulnerable to disruption in the new era of globalization. If it operates primarily within the legal regime governing one bloc, but has a large base of customers in a bloc with an incongruous legal regime, again, things are likely to become increasingly complex in the coming years. Conversely, firms more exclusively entrenched in a single bloc may now maintain advantages over their more diversified neighbors.

All of this is to say that the corporate world's decades-long focus on building just-in-time dynamics will increasingly shift to the imperatives of "just in case." Put another way: the premium once placed on efficiency is being balanced with a new focus on resilience. Global data centers are being replaced by smaller regional or country-specific ones. Capital is being raised more frequently in home markets or by those who are friendly with a company's home government. And logistics and supply chain attributes that were once viewed as unalloyed virtues—the cost savings borne from maintaining minimal inventory and cultivating the lowest-cost suppliers, without much regard for how far-flung they were—now have to be balanced against the economic and, especially, political benefits of producing locally.

RISK AND OPPORTUNITY

What will this shift mean for corporate executives? The answer will vary from one C-suite to the next, but in many cases, the shake-up will require management teams to think anew when making decisions big and small. For the last 30 years, many management teams have been given a broad license to gloss over geopolitical dynamics explicitly because certain fundamentals could broadly be taken for granted. But the next era of globalization will rip away that luxury. Executives will not be able to ignore the tectonic changes underway, even as they are still compelled to compete on the fronts that dominated their concerns throughout the last 30 years.

The return of the geostrategic imperative will force executives to face a series of more fundamental questions: In the face of uncertainty, will your company sit back to see how things evolve? Alternatively, will you follow Toyota's lead, working to get ahead of the curve? Framed in those terms, the choice may appear obvious—better to be proactive than reactive. But given all the ongoing shifts in geopolitical architecture, it will be tempting to hold steady, to let others take what may turn out to be foolish risks, and to preserve what your company has for fear of losing too much on a risky mistake.

But we believe it's a mistake to give in to the temptation in a moment like this, to hunker down as you're buffeted by changes from nearly every direction. The issue is whether executives have the right information to make informed decisions before they are entirely certain about how the winds are blowing. Can they collect enough intelligence to make the sorts of educated guesses Toyota's executives made in the 1980s and 1990s? Can they parse the data to give them more insight into how the world is likely to shift before the competition does?

That's why successful executives will begin investing in new strategies to understand global dynamics early. The secret to Toyota's success wasn't just its leadership's willingness to take risks—it was also the company's investment in gauging how geopolitical dynamics could create new opportunities for the business. That capacity is lacking in many companies today. To close that gap, companies need to invest much more heavily in the practice of geostrategy—the holistic and cross-functional integration of political risk management into broader risk management, strategy, and governance.

During the next era of globalization, executives will be judged by a standard slightly different from that which prevailed in decades past. Shareholders will, of course, still care about quarterly figures—revenues, profits, and future projections—moving forward. And a broader set of stakeholders will still focus on ESG issues. But increasingly, CEOs and other executives will also be measured by their geostrategic acumen because shifting geopolitical circumstances will have more material impacts on business outcomes. That is to say, not only will executives need to prove their mettle by meeting the sorts of changes that defined the post–Cold War global order—they'll also need to show they have the savvy to navigate much more uncertain political terrain as well.

In the new era of globalization, geostrategic imperatives will affect both short-term profits and long-term value creation. In the immediate aftermath of Russia's decision to invade Ukraine in early 2022, media coverage tended to focus on the first-order economic impacts—primarily Europe's scramble to find alternative sources for the energy it had long purchased from Russia. Almost entirely ignored initially were second-order impacts: *other* raw materials needed for clean energy technology—including so-called "green" critical minerals, such as nickel and cobalt—were also put at a new premium, because Russia was the source of so much of the globe's supply at 11 percent and 5 percent, respectively. And eastern Ukraine may contain as much as 500,000 tons of lithium oxide, constituting one of the largest global deposits. But, amid the fighting, these supplies were broadly inaccessible. [9, 10, 11]

That's a near-perfect encapsulation of the new premium executives will need to put on their companies' capacity to anticipate and pivot in response to geopolitical change. In the years and decades to come, businesses that once presumed a level of stability in the markets for oil and gas—not to mention for nickel and cobalt—will be caught flat-footed if they're blind to geopolitical dynamics. This points to another element of the new era of globalization: governments in the future are likely to play much more proactive roles in shaping economic realities through export bans, investment restrictions, and other industrial policies. And that means that regardless of how much companies invested in their governments and public affairs teams, tomorrow's executives will need to have much more insight into what's happening along the corridors of political power.

That new reality was made clear through the pandemic. When societies around the world suddenly found themselves competing for supplies of personal protective equipment, pharmaceuticals, and the materials enabling their production and distribution (e.g., vials), the shortcomings of the previous regime of globalization came into stark relief. Public figures governing countries that had become dependent on foreign production suddenly began to put a new premium on self-sufficiency. Imported goods, they realized, might be more affordable. But the new geopolitical reality meant that many were willing to pay a premium for goods and services from domestic sources that might otherwise be in short supply.

Consider this: over the course of the last decade, there has been a fairly steady crescendo of trade and investment barriers. Governments have implemented more than

40,000 discriminatory trade interventions since November of 2008—compared with just over 9,000 liberalizing policy interventions.[12] Populism recently reached its highest peak since the Second World War.[13] Supply chain disruptions born from terrorist incidents have lopped off as much as 9 percent of stock market capitalization.[14] And together, these various risks are driving up the cost of capital.[15]

The point here is that these geopolitical complications layer one on top of the other. Concerns about energy security will bleed into adoption of emerging technologies. The increased use of AI may provide new avenues for cyberterrorism and state-sponsored cyberattacks. Efforts to build up national self-sufficiency will affect manufacturers, automakers, life sciences companies, agribusiness, and renewable energy companies, among others.

These complications are not only sirens executives should not ignore—in many cases, there are opportunities hidden in the fog. They will inevitably play a crucial role in determining tomorrow's winners and losers. This is why geostrategy is now such a necessity. Executives made aware early of the heightened risk of war between neighboring countries might prepare, for example, by supplementing manufacturing facilities elsewhere to head off a potential disruption in the future. Those given an early sense that trade barriers might fall between two erstwhile adversaries might consider a merger that otherwise made little economic sense. A C-suite informed of a false rumor circulating on social media in one foreign market might shift an advertising campaign to head off future trouble. But all of these scenarios, which are likely to become more frequent in the future, depend on a company's ability to scan, focus, and act upon real intelligence as it comes in. And that requires a level of insight that many C-suites have yet to acquire.

PUTTING GEOSTRATEGY INTO PRACTICE

Geostrategy may be rising to become an imperative in the new era of globalization, but much of the corporate world is still struggling to figure out how to get it right. Companies that spent years, if not decades, maintaining teams capable of keeping their supply chains efficient haven't built up the capacity to monitor geopolitical shifts, let alone anticipate those changes and pivot strategies accordingly. While businesses might know today how to navigate a complex merger or overhaul their finances or spin-off a subsidiary, very few executives are experienced in setting up systems capable of providing actionable, political risk intelligence to company decision-makers on an ongoing basis.

Geostrategy requires a different toolbox. And it requires a specific skill set. To understand the world as it's evolving, a company needs to establish trusted sources of political risk intelligence. Executives need to be able to unpack how any newly identified shifts may affect their operations, investments, workforce, and other areas of the business. And finally, companies need to be able to act in real time, ensuring that those making decisions about a company's global investments and operational decisions reflect what the intelligence suggests is likely to happen. And that means that the process must be regularized and professionalized.

We are only now in the early stages of this transition. To this point, less than a third of companies engage in a proactive approach to managing political risk, while 40 percent have an ad hoc or reactive approach.[16] But, in the years and decades to come, that will have to shift. Executives will begin to see how other firms have used geostrategy to their advantage. Some CEOs will be lauded for being ahead of the curve, and others will be criticized for having dropped the ball. So, right now is a critical moment for C-suites across the world—an opportunity to determine the nuts and bolts of designing and implementing a geostrategy ahead of their competitors.

No two companies will embrace precisely the same approach because geostrategy needs to be tailored to each company's organization and culture. But generally, companies should follow a five-step process, outlined below, to build an effective geostrategic capability. Across industries and sectors, we've found this to be leading practice.

1. **Identify and dynamically monitor political risks.** Given the current shift in the global operating environment and the elevated level of political risks around the world, executives should invest in improved identification and dynamic monitoring of political risks to enhance their understanding of the geopolitical environment. Political risks should be included as part of a company's risk register or other risk identification processes and must be dynamically monitored on an ongoing basis. Also, while political risk will always involve qualitative analysis, companies should collect and integrate quantitative

indicators into their political risk identification and monitoring systems.

2. **Assess how these political risks could affect your company.** Executives should strengthen their company's ability to conduct political risk impact assessments at the functional or business unit level. These functional or business unit impact assessments should also inform an enterprise-wide assessment of potential political risk impacts on a regular basis. In parallel, executives should conduct a top-down assessment at the corporate level. Companies can model the potential impacts of various political risk events across key business functions, such as revenue, supply chain, investments, and data management.

3. **Integrate political risk into connected risk approaches.** Executives should integrate political risk into their company's risk management process to gain a more holistic view of the outside risks that they face. Such integration is particularly impactful if it leverages the political risk identification outputs and the tangible estimations of political risk impact developed in steps one and two. The team responsible for managing political risk should seek to target financial and operational hedging strategies that help minimize the impact of downside political risk events, while also proactively identifying strategic opportunities the company could pursue related to upside political risk events.

4. **Incorporate political risk analysis into strategic decisions.** Executives should task the geostrategic team with conducting a global footprint assessment for political risks—and then adjust their footprint strategy accordingly. They should also proactively include political risk analysis in strategic planning processes, including market entry and exit, M&A, and other transactions. Given the current uncertainty associated with the trajectory of globalization, one leading practice is to use scenario analysis to inform strategic decisions. Executives should be actively involved in these processes to demonstrate that there is buy-in from the top regarding the importance of incorporating political risk into company culture and strategic decisions.

5. **Establish a cross-functional geostrategic team.** Finally, executives need to ensure political risk management is communicated and coordinated across the company. One effective way to do this is to establish a cross-functional geostrategic team that includes representatives who engage in geostrategy from the political, operational, risk management, and strategic perspectives. Members should come from both the C-suite and relevant functions and business units. The team should meet on a regular cadence to discuss the political risks the company faces, how and where those risks are likely to impact the business, and what the company is and should be doing to manage them. This team should also report to the CEO and board of directors on a regular basis.

THIS BOOK

The shift away from the norms that prevailed throughout the post–Cold War era represents a watershed rife with both risk and opportunity. To thrive, executives will have to avoid the temptation to shrink away, taking instead a proactive approach to managing geopolitical shifts, including understanding their likely impacts and empowering their enterprises to pivot expeditiously as the globe's architecture continues to evolve.

The chapters that follow, each of which relates to one item on the five-point agenda above, were written to help executives navigate the geopolitical uncertainty they currently face by guiding their efforts to establish a regularized, professionalized geostrategy. These five steps correspond with the five parts of the EY Geostrategy Framework (see figure 1). These chapters

FIGURE 1.

THE EY GEOSTRATEGY FRAMEWORK FOR STRATEGIC POLITICAL RISK MANAGEMENT

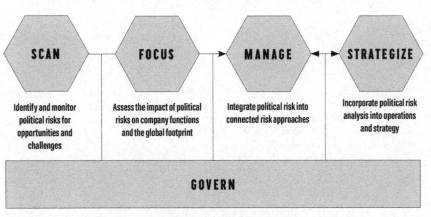

SCAN	FOCUS	MANAGE	STRATEGIZE
Identify and monitor political risks for opportunities and challenges	Assess the impact of political risks on company functions and the global footprint	Integrate political risk into connected risk approaches	Incorporate political risk analysis into operations and strategy

GOVERN

Establish a cross-functional geostrategic team based on the fundamentals of ownership, communication, and trust

Source: EY Geostrategic Business Group.

dive much deeper into the five elements required and the various steps within each that an executive team should take to make geostrategy a strength rather than a vulnerability. It will not be an easy task—but it's crucial. Any company determined to thrive in the decades to come will need to incorporate dynamics shaping the new era of globalization into their strategy. And that's exactly what geostrategy is equipped to do.

1

SCAN

Identify and dynamically monitor political risks

Never before in history has it been so easy for executives to access such a wide array of data, so many types of analysis, and such a diverse collection of perspectives. But as every executive knows, that great gift is also an enormous burden. The unrelenting deluge of information requires C-suites to invest more effort in trying to separate various signals from the noise. And in a world where change is constant—one in which global risks and opportunities evolve so rapidly— there's a new premium on finding the *right* information and doing so *quickly*. That's why geostrategy begins with an endeavor we call "scan."

Scan goes beyond simply collecting more information—it encompasses more crucially the work required to see the forest from the trees. To seize opportunities and manage risk, executive teams and boards need to place individual shifts within the broader geopolitical context. And that means not only finding good sources of information, but also contextualizing them within the broader framework of what is often breathless news coverage. In the absence of a good scan function within their companies, executives are more likely to misread a signal or overreact to blips of news. And that can have grave consequences. Miss a risk, and a company is liable to step blindly into a crisis; overstate one, and a company may overlook a potential opportunity. And yet, despite its importance, scan remains scattershot and haphazard throughout much of the corporate world. That needs to change.

Consider, as one illustration of the challenges companies face when trying to get scan right, the degree to which many companies failed to anticipate the Asian financial crisis of the late 1990s. Born primarily of the fact that several East Asian governments were investing in speculative projects while simultaneously maintaining what turned out to be unsustainable currency pegs, the great curiosity, in retrospect, is that so few analysts within the global financial community identified the underlying risks at the time. No scan can pick up every conceivable risk. But in the years leading up to the crisis, countries ranging from Thailand to Indonesia were sitting on a giant bubble that, when it popped, posed downside risks to companies around the globe.

The question many executives asked afterward was how the problem had gone undetected for so long. And the answer was remarkable: although these various Asian economies were purportedly being scrutinized by analysts, investors, and journalists, many observers had seemingly missed what was really going on regarding the buildup of financial risks. Companies that had invested in these economies were left to deal with the consequences of risks that many of their executives had not fully considered. In most cases, that wasn't because C-suites had ignored them—rather, they'd been caught blind.

Scan failures can overstate risks as well. In the wake of a corruption scandal in Brazil that led to the iconic "Car Wash" anti-corruption investigation, initiated in March 2014, two reflections for Brazil's legal and economic environment stood out. The first is related to the enforcement of the Brazilian Anti-Bribery Law, or Clean Companies Act, promulgated in 2013 and designed to uproot other instances of corruption. This law received significant international media attention as a result of the discovery of the corruption scheme. The second is that the corruption scandal had a significant negative effect on the global perception of Brazil as a haven for graft, chilling global interest in Brazil and, in some cases, its Latin American neighbors. The perception of heightened risk steered global capital to other opportunities.

Through the years, as the "Car Wash" investigation worked feverishly to root out corruption, the unit's various investigations ended up convicting hundreds of people and returning R$4.3 billion (about US$803 million) to public coffers.[17] But, on the whole, the results seemed to indicate that corruption was actually less prevalent than had been assumed by many observers (even though indicators, such as the Corruptions Perception Index, highlight continuing corruption issues in Brazil). This pointed to a sobering conclusion: companies that had chosen not to incorporate Brazilian manufacturing in their supply chains, or that had declined opportunities to merge or acquire Brazilian firms, had potentially passed up what could have been lucrative business ventures.

Again, the problem in both episodes was not that the information required to make informed judgments was not available—in both cases, the underlying reality could have been discerned if scan functions had been more robust. That underlying problem—namely executives' lack of an accurate picture of what was happening on the ground—had been born from three separate challenges, all of which were endemic through the early post–Cold War period: a lack of demand for political risk intelligence, an inadequate process for scanning the political risk environment, and a dearth of supply of such analyses.

Understanding those three elements—and, perhaps more importantly, how circumstances are changing in all three respects—can help executives put in place a more sophisticated and useful approach to scanning for political risks. The good news is that, if done systematically, we now have tools to vastly improve the information gathering and analysis most companies rely on to succeed. But to get the best results, companies need to make the process rigorous, sophisticated, and complete.

THE INCOMPLETE SCAN

In previous eras, the C-suite was markedly less interested in high-quality geostrategic insights—and, in many cases, for good reason. Throughout the 1990s, many executives saw little value in paying close attention to the political risks of global expansion. Looking back, that makes some intuitive sense. In the years that followed the Berlin Wall's collapse, crises with global ramifications were few and far between—there was an economic boom until the late 1990s, and the overall geopolitical system was relatively stable.

But that balance was upended recently. Now, political risks tend to be more correlated across markets. Think about the wave of social unrest that spread across countries during the Arab Spring of 2010 and 2011, or the rise of populist politicians across Europe and other regions in the 2000s and 2010s.[18, 19] At the same time, systemic geopolitical risks are affecting many markets and sectors around the world— with the war in Ukraine being a case in point. The stakes have thus been raised. And that argues for taking the first step toward establishing a more sophisticated geostrategy: improving a company's ability to collect, discern, and interpret meaningful information.

As globalization evolves, C-suites will continue to grapple with increasing government intervention, including the push for supply chain resilience and limiting market access, and ESG dynamics. Whether these political risks translate into opportunities or challenges will depend, in many cases, on how and when companies identify them. That then reflects a broader shift: quality insights increasingly come at a higher premium. Accurate political risk analysis will become a more powerful competitive advantage, so demand for political risk scans will continue to rise.

The second reason scan has been neglected centers on the reality that companies haven't done it well. For example, many firms began relying on the opinions of (sometimes underqualified) "specialists" responding to queries about the business climates in various countries around the world. Even quantitative measures were based on qualitative surveys. As a result, impressions gleaned from people with individual biases, and who sometimes had limited insight, informed executives' impressions of risk and opportunity.

Scan processes often gave too much credence to the rarefied wisdom of former government officials brought in to sit on a board or join an advisory panel. The EY *Geostrategy in Practice 2020* survey revealed that over three-quarters of global companies (76 percent) recruit individuals with political experience to fill board or senior leadership positions.[20] There's no doubt that many of these individuals have a great deal to teach a company—offering insights into the minds of key leaders, how processes work within governments, and the underlying sources of geopolitical tensions. But, in some cases, their retrospective impressions of what prevailed in the previous era of globalization are not sufficient in today's era of global flux.

And that points to a critical problem with the legacy process of scanning for political risks: it has generally been backward-looking, using lagging indicators to extrapolate what would likely happen in the future. At a moment when CEOs are so keenly aware that, as the financial admonition goes, "past performance is no guarantee of future earnings," retrospective analysis is not a suitable method for understanding political risks in various markets within a changing world. The pace of globalization's evolution demands something more rigorous and forward-looking.

The most salient reason scan has been so deficient in the past is likely the lack of supply. In previous eras, there were only a limited number of political risk sources available, and most of them were purely qualitative analysis. That challenge speaks to the fundamental imperative, namely getting the right information from a comprehensive scan and communicating it effectively throughout a company. So, to correct for previous deficiencies, executives need to craft systems and infrastructure equipped to identify the right signal amid the geopolitical noise. The good news is that, today, they can.

SCAN DONE RIGHT

Scanning for political risk might appear to be simple—just compile all the data and organize it. But the process is a combination of art and science. Disaggregating the most important information from any swirl of contradictory *qualitative* information and analysis requires savvy, discipline, and skill. And picking out the right *quantitative* data requires familiarity with both international and local sources. Although scan can be tricky, a company that follows a structured and rigorous process is much more likely to cull useful intelligence for the C-suite. Below, we highlight the five elements geostrategy teams should embrace to do scan right.

1. Define and segment the universe of political risks

First, geostrategy teams need to establish a scan template that invites those monitoring the world to be widely expansive in their search for information. That means, most importantly, creating categories that cast a wide net, encompassing the full range of political risk—the political decisions, events, and conditions at the geopolitical, country, regulatory, and societal levels that might impact the performance of a company, market, or economy (see figure 2). "Risk," in this context, should encompass both downside and upside developments. By establishing a limited but comprehensive and interlinked number of buckets, analysts are less likely to overlook important developments—and they're more apt to identify cross-cutting concerns.

With the universe of political risks established, analysts should begin with a thorough scan of what we call **geopolitical risks**—namely those that emerge when alliances shift, when the interests of countries in defined policy areas collide, or when the international system at large is undergoing transformation. In a break from stability that defined the post–Cold War era, these sorts of geopolitical shifts have intensified more recently because of the evolving global dynamics surrounding the increasingly complex relationships between three great powers—the US, the EU, and China. At the same time, a variety of geopolitical swing states have more sway than in the past. And the Bretton Woods multilateral institutions are beginning to play reduced roles on the global stage, creating a more volatile and uncertain geopolitical environment governed by smaller, overlapping institutions.

These new geopolitical dynamics will play out differently for various firms and industries. Sectors deemed strategic for economic or national security reasons—semiconductors, AI, EVs, pharmaceuticals, and critical infrastructure, among others—are likely to face export controls, restrictive trade measures, and increased limitations on (or rejections

FIGURE 2.
SCAN: IDENTIFY AND DYNAMICALLY MONITOR POLITICAL RISKS ACROSS FOUR LEVELS

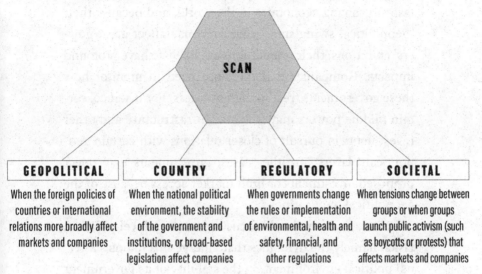

GEOPOLITICAL	COUNTRY	REGULATORY	SOCIETAL
When the foreign policies of countries or international relations more broadly affect markets and companies	When the national political environment, the stability of the government and institutions, or broad-based legislation affect companies	When governments change the rules or implementation of environmental, health and safety, financial, and other regulations	When tensions change between groups or when groups launch public activism (such as boycotts or protests) that affects markets and companies

Source: EY Geostrategic Business Group.

of) cross-border investment. Governments may more frequently pursue global competitiveness through trade policy interventions in corporate supply chains.

The proliferation of geopolitical risks will have significant business implications. Chinese companies seeking to operate or raise capital in the US, for example, may face regulatory and reputational challenges at home. US firms operating in China may find it increasingly difficult to navigate between the two markets. Rather than exit either market, many companies are likely to seek to manage these reputational risks—but that won't be easy.

Geopolitical risk and opportunity will also shift for middle powers—countries that play an outsized role shaping geopolitics within their regions or on a global scale, but which individually wield less influence than great powers. Because middle powers include some of the largest and fastest-growing economies in the world, and because their "geopolitical swing state" character may affect great powers' ambitions, their orientations are likely to have profound impacts. Companies will therefore need to monitor how these governments treat foreign business. For instance, certain middle powers may welcome infrastructure and other investments in pursuit of closer relations with certain geopolitical players; in other cases, governments may reject proposed investments or limit market access because of the geopolitical implications.

Next, analysts should focus on **country-level political risks**, namely the dynamics that emerge in a nation's internal political environment, in the stability of its government and institutions, and in broad-based legislation that will have measurable economic consequences. Elections and leadership transitions are the most prominent example of country-level political risk, because they can so profoundly affect a country's overall policy agenda. Climate policy is an example of one such area that has been volatile due to heightened country risk.

The US, Australia, and several other countries drastically changed their approaches to climate policy after recent elections, and they and other countries may do the same after future government transitions. Subsequent governments have enhanced, changed, or withdrawn various policies designed to reduce carbon emissions or unleash new revenue streams. Other countries are likely to launch big-ticket policy reforms to introduce carbon pricing or reduce the consumption of natural resources. Many will try to incentivize the use of renewable energy sources or boost new, low-carbon products and processes. These policies will add both direct and indirect operating costs across sectors, while also providing growth opportunities for some companies and sectors. Governments may also shift the ways they provide sustainability tax incentives for companies and households, opening the door for companies to finance green R&D or their own energy transitions.

Third, a comprehensive geostrategy demands a scan of **regulatory risks**, namely those that emerge when governments at the international, national, or local level change the rules or implementation of environmental, health and safety, financial market, and other standards. Quite often, a regulation imposed in one part of the world influences the decisions made elsewhere, even if there isn't a direct tie. The EU's General Data Protection Regulation (GDPR), for instance, has had an extraterritorial effect on foreign companies doing business in or with the EU market. Regulatory risks can also spread globally through the so-called Brussels Effect, a phenomenon epitomized by the GDPR, which inspired other governments around the world to enact similar, but sometimes distinct, policies focused on digital privacy. We're seeing something similar play out now with AI regulations.

When governments impose new regulations, this often raises costs and complicates business models—but it can also create opportunities. As an example, take the potential Brussels Effect of the EU's recent sustainability regulations. Even before being subject to new demands from domestic regulators, companies with low emissions in their supply chains may enjoy competitive advantages elsewhere around the world. And heightened transparency and reporting standards may pose both downside and upside reputational risks for companies, depending on their levels of transparency, accountability, and progress on sustainability metrics. Knowing that, some companies are using the potential for new regulations to begin tracking sustainability metrics on a voluntary basis.

Fourth, geostrategists need to monitor what we call **societal risks.** These include when tensions change between societal groups or when the dynamics that emerge when groups, ranging from trade unions to consumer bodies, launch public activism designed to exert pressure on companies or markets. Societal risks have also been on the rise in recent years. We've seen the rise of international social activism, such as the FridaysForFuture environmental protests and the "me too." women's rights movement. Global billionaires' wealth rose by more than 27 percent during the pandemic, even while approximately 120 million people were pushed into extreme poverty.[21, 22] That societal dynamic played out differently in different places, but in general it raised the risk of social unrest and political instability. Similar sorts of ripples are likely to unfold as global energy and food prices rise in the future.

Societal risks often spur governments to embrace redistributive measures—policies designed to provide new social services, create middle-class jobs, or impose new taxes on wealthy individuals and corporations. This frequently creates new political risks—both upside and downside. In the US, for instance, societal activism may eventually drive support for childcare subsidies, and those reforms may spur more parents (especially mothers) to return to the labor force, expanding the domestic economy's talent pool. Elsewhere, societal shifts may compel cash-strapped or highly indebted governments to raise corporate taxes.

The absence of government attention to inequities can pose even more dangerous and unpredictable political risks. For instance, marginalized groups can engage in large-scale demonstrations or even violent conflict. Persistent inequality can lead to voters supporting more extreme or populist political leaders and policies.

These four interconnected categories serve as a good starting point for a company's geostrategy team to conduct a comprehensive political risk scan. By delineating these differences, they impose a discipline and structure on the scanning process and outputs. Without thinking through all four, scanners are apt to miss important developments. In the scan process, the core danger is myopia. Establishing these clear metrics will help to ensure a more comprehensive effort by geostrategists and enhance the ability to collect all the relevant information.

2. Collect political risk insights from a variety of sources

Once a company has settled on its definitions of political risk, the firm's geostrategists can begin their search. Of course, geostrategy teams cannot identify and monitor *all* political risks around the world. While scanning widely is best practice, it is not required to scan for everything. Geostrategists should focus on the political risks in markets and issue areas that are material to their company. This concept of materiality is something we'll explore in more detail in the Focus chapter. The point here is to be as expansive as possible, knowing that whatever universe of risks initially makes the cut, the firm will have an opportunity to dive in more deeply down the road.

Companies with extensive political competency—those, for example, that have a robust government affairs arm—may already understand many of the political risks facing their business. But to do scan right, the whole organization needs to be involved, both by feeding information to the centralized team and, as we'll see later, by consuming the collected intelligence. This will be a shift even for some of the most sophisticated firms, but it is imperative that political risk analysis does not get siloed.

According to a recent survey, almost two-thirds of companies rely primarily on enterprise-level identification of emerging risks.[23] But depending solely on such a top-down process can create blind spots if dispersed, bottom-up observations and intelligence from across markets, functions, and business units aren't included in a firm's comprehensive geostrategic scan. If those more nuanced insights are withheld from those trying to scan and map a company's political risks, executives are likely to miss important developments.[24] Creating a comprehensive roster of possible risks is a massive undertaking, and those in charge of managing the process need to begin with both bottom-up and top-down processes.

For that reason, firms shouldn't look exclusively inward for data and information. Scanners should also monitor a range of external sources, including periodicals, reports, and other reliable sources of published intelligence. And they should make sure to talk to people on the ground in the markets they serve and in the places where they do business. To that end, geostrategists in certain industries may be able to broaden their scans by engaging trade associations and interest groups. The Pharmaceutical Manufacturing Forum (PMF), for example, conducts studies that provide participating life science companies with a wealth of geostrategic information, including what new regulations may be imminent in various countries and which trade blocs may be poised to restrict the export of intellectual property.[25]

Analysts can also supplement homegrown and shared intelligence from outside professionals. Some analytical firms are well equipped to add qualitative data, having deployed their own staff on the ground in various places throughout the world. Others will have more skill culling high-quality quantitative data that unearths emerging risks, which would otherwise go unnoticed. Whomever a firm might engage, the hope is that this broader range of perspectives will not only reveal new upside and downside risks, but that it will also provide divergent perspectives on risks the firm has already identified.

We have found it is important to braid qualitative and quantitative intelligence together in any comprehensive analysis (see figure 3). Some have come to view qualitative sources—articles, interviews, and notions passed on in sidebar conversations—as passé or unreliable. And it's true that, where possible, geostrategy teams should bring quantitative indicators to bear, such as tariff rates, corruption levels, tax rates, Gini coefficients, and more innovative metrics. But quantitative data can leave holes in a scan—geopolitics is complex, idiosyncratic, and dynamic. So, it's in this combination of different sources of information that blind spots are most likely to come into clear view.

Braiding together the two approaches to information gathering can also spur further inquiry. If, for example, a scanner hears from sources on the ground that certain demographic groups are upset with a prevailing regime, but key polling indicators haven't changed in any notable way, that would be a prompt for further investigation. Perhaps polls that missed coming political unrest are overlooking other important data as well. Perhaps the qualitative sources aren't seeing the full picture. Whatever the case may be, discrepancies in the information uncovered in the scan can serve as red flags.

FIGURE 3.
SCAN: BRAIDING TOGETHER DIFFERENT SOURCES OF POLITICAL RISK ANALYSIS

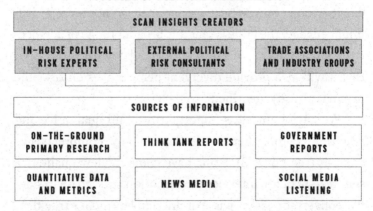

Source: Adapted from Jon Shames, Mary Karol Cline, Witold J. Henisz, "How to improve political risk management: Interviews with global executives reveal the need for balance between political, operational and financial management strategies," EY and the Political Risk Lab at the Wharton School, University of Pennsylvania, February 2021.

In the end, the key to bringing all these elements together is geostrategic experience and skill. Those analyzing tranches of data and reading reams of reports need sufficient capabilities to analyze multiple sources of information and draw the right conclusions. For example, reports emerged in 2022 that a group of European lawmakers were advocating for the EU to reject green gas and nuclear investment rules.[26] A good scanner would have taken notice of the reports, but avoided a knee-jerk reaction, and instead would have dug into the issue to assess the likelihood of those lawmakers being successful. This would have avoided an unnecessary response since, in the end, that particular group of lawmakers did not have sufficient support to prevail. The EU did end up including nuclear and gas energy activities in its taxonomy for sustainable activities.[27] Geostrategy is refined by experience such that more seasoned scanners can quickly distinguish how to respond to multiple information sources and when to explore signals further.

3. Assess the likelihood of the political risks that were identified

Next, analysts should assess the likelihood that various political risks will present themselves within a particular timeframe. That means moving beyond identifying the existence of an underlying risk to assessing the probability that it will actually come into play. We sometimes refer to this as the "Volcano Dilemma." Someone living on a volcanic island likely knows that the lava could pour out of the crater at any given time. But what matters is not that the volcano *could* erupt, but *whether and when* it will. What matters is how active the fault line is likely to be. In much the same way, geostrategy requires not just the identification of potential challenges and opportunities, but also an assessment of their likelihood over the time period relevant to executives' decision-making about company operations and strategy.

The Volcano Dilemma applies in a wide range of circumstances. It goes without saying that societies around the world are awash with a whole range of tensions across classes, ethnicities, political parties, and much more. But, in many cases, those tensions are unlikely to manifest as a political risk event. Risk analysis, then, should include both a structural baseline for stability *and* "red flags" that affect the likelihood of a given outcome. It's not that risks *can't* happen if they're deemed unlikely—a purportedly dormant volcano could indeed erupt without warning. It's just that the two elements of any analysis are distinct and need to be considered separately.

Consider, as an illustration, the divergent outcomes from Kenya's presidential elections in 2018 and 2022. Kenyan society sits atop a kind of demographic volcano; the country's population is divided by a range of tribal identities. But while those underlying tensions are age-old, the impacts vary from one moment to the next. A wave of violence spilled onto Kenya's streets after a leader hailing from one tribe lost the 2018 presidential contest. But when the very same politician came up short four years later, relative calm prevailed. The underlying fault line remained the same, but the short-term societal risks affecting the level of activity along that fault line differed.

Here's where a more experienced scanner would earn their keep: a deeper dive would have pulled together evidence from before 2018, revealing why violence was more likely in the wake of Kenya's election, and would subsequently have revealed that, because the leading candidates disavowed violence and reinforced trust in the electoral system and other institutions, it was less apt to emerge in 2022. The value of any scan is burnished by having a depth of knowledge that gauges not only the underlying tension in a society, but what might be termed the "likelihood of manifestation" at a given time.

Finally, the geostrategy team must be proficient at making connections between various risks and opportunities, determining how the likelihood of one political risk may affect another. How could a volcano erupting on one island affect seismic activity on another island? To hearken back to a previous illustration, Russia's 2022 invasion of Ukraine not only changed the contours of global oil and gas markets—but it also put a premium on some of the raw materials required for green energy production and electrification. That, in turn, led to a series of industrial policies promoting exploration and production of green minerals in a variety of countries around the world. In essence, a geopolitical event that appeared to bear most heavily on Eastern Europe also had enormous implications elsewhere around the world. A good scan will make those sorts of connections such that, when an event *does* occur, a company understands the ripple effects.

There is no magic formula here in the same way there's no precise way to train a doctor's brain to diagnose an illness in the absence of perfect information. Experience matters, and a good physician knows how to make informed guesses. But that's why professionalizing scan, and having an established process in place around it, makes it more of an art form than a science. In much the same way that an experienced scanner would have known that the European Parliament's proposed rules on including gas and nuclear energy activities in the sustainability taxonomy were destined to pass, proficient geostrategists develop a nose for unearthing the most important trends.

4. Monitor and reassess continuously

The geostrategic scanner's job is never done. Their work must be perpetual and dynamic—not periodic. Geostrategists must avoid the pitfall that marginalizes the benefits of scan, namely relegating it to a rote process tacked on to an annual review. Scanning once a year—or even once a quarter—will not serve to improve operational and strategic decision-making. To catch emerging risks in real time, analysts always need to have their antennae outstretched and their noses to the ground. A company that completed a scan in December 2021 might not have included the ripple effects born out of the war in Ukraine. But once the war began, they would have needed to pivot. For that reason, executives acting on intelligence gained from scans done even just six months before are compelled to work off what is often obsolete intelligence, particularly in the dynamic geopolitical environment that prevails today.

That said, having too much information—too many reports to read, indictors to monitor, and conversations to process—can drive a different set of problems. Once a geostrategist is more familiarized with the landscape, a savvy scanner will be able to discard less useful reports and data points with more alacrity, allowing for a scan process that is both faster and more useful. The key, in the end, isn't simply to intake all the information, but to glean useful information from the deluge on an ongoing basis. We discuss relevant backgrounds and profiles for such geostrategists in the Govern chapter. But the salient point for now is that this competency is built and honed over time.

5. Share insights regularly and in real time

The final step centers on the output—namely in distributing the insights from a complete scan. It is critical to get the cadence and design of this communication right. Even the highest-quality analysis won't move the needle if its insights are lost on the decision-makers shaping a company's operations and strategy. That means that effective geostrategists must not only collect information from across the company. They must also parse their analysis into deliverables useful to a wide variety of stakeholders. This balance requires a two-way flow of information between the geostrategy team and business decision-makers. Executives and other stakeholders need then to take seriously the insights born from geostrategic scan—to operationalize them as part of whatever corporate function they inhabit.

This means that political analysis must not only be used by a company's government affairs team. It must be incorporated through financial models, dashboards, and metrics that facilitate coordination across a variety of functions and business units. If scanners highlight the downside political risks associated with entering a new market, but the transaction team executes the deal without a mitigation plan for those risks, the company could suffer a significant loss on that investment. Every decision-maker across the whole company must receive geostrategic analysis on a regular basis in a form that empowers them to leverage the relevant insights. Doing this well requires assessments of the impact of political risk on companies—a process we'll explore in more detail in the next chapter.

Executives we speak with often point to information challenges associated with geostrategy teams. For instance, they would like to receive more accurate data sooner, but the highly contextual nature of political risk and the complex forces that give rise to it mean that information can sometimes prove to be too little, too late. Strategizing with imperfect information is often seen as an unavoidable challenge of political risk management.

The point here is that scanners must maintain real and deep relationships with both the people feeding them insights based on unique experiences and perspectives from across the company, and those consuming and acting on geostrategic reports. Often, building these sorts of ties between scanners and the rest of the organization requires more effort than is first expected—but the payoff is clear. Real integration helps sharpen everyone's understanding of where political risk insight can play a role in managing broader strategic questions.

In essence, geostrategic scans are only valuable if they effectively help decision-makers understand the macro themes driving political risk events and the broader context for developments. Without regular contact with the firm's geostrategists, executives are too often drawn to focus on the "urgent" rather than the "important." But if they *are* in more frequent touch with those tasked with leading a company's scan, small, identified changes can quickly be translated into useful insights that bear directly on an executive's decisions. As one scanner explained to us when discussing this subject, "It's very easy to be interesting; it's much harder to be useful." But that, of course, is the goal—to help the company make better geostrategic decisions.

THE BENEFITS OF SCAN

During the first half of 2022, EY teams helped a company to engage in what can only be described as an emergency scan. The company, which maintains a footprint in markets around the world, had settled on a strategy to expand sales in China. That decision comported with the broadly held notion that China was poised to be a key driver of business growth in the twenty-first century for two obvious reasons: first, the country's population is enormous. Second, that enormous population has become increasingly prosperous as tens of millions of people rise out of rural poverty and into the country's growing, and increasingly urban, middle class.

The client had crafted a comprehensive strategy, which would require the construction of several large manufacturing plants in China that would serve Chinese consumers. The company also planned to develop large-scale facilities to enable them to do more research within China. But, then, having hatched this growth strategy for China years earlier, several executives in the company began to second-guess the wisdom of the move. No single precipitating factor led them to develop cold feet. Rather, these doubts occurred as a reaction to a series of red flags that spurred the executive team to reconsider.

Daunted by what was clearly a high-stakes decision, they sought our help. They wanted a better understanding of how things would play out if they moved forward—and if they decided to switch course. So, we began with a blank slate and tried to paint a picture, not only identifying the fault lines, but also tackling the Volcano Dilemma—namely gauging the likelihood that any given dynamic was likely to come into play in the relevant time horizon. In the end, our client needed a way of considering the broad matrix of political risks in a comprehensive way—an issue scan was explicitly created to address.

The scan was conducted across the four categories outlined above. To identify individual risks, we asked a range of pointed questions: Would regulators restrict the prices the company could charge when selling products to Chinese consumers, limiting revenue and profit opportunities? What was the likelihood that some organizations would try to take possession of the company's intellectual property? Would the company's status as a Western corporation end up being a liability? Would there be measures to prevent local data, gleaned from research performed within China, from being integrated into global data sets? How would geopolitical developments such as the war in Ukraine affect operations in China?

We were, of course, unable to answer any of these questions with absolute certainty—that's beyond the power of scan. But we were able to bring some clarity to the broader political risk landscape. To shape our answers, we spoke with several stakeholders in the company, each with their own perspectives on the issues. We consulted professionals on China from around the world, many of whom had more specific knowledge in what was happening in Beijing. We invited professionals inside the global EY organization to the table to discuss what was happening in the company's sector globally—how other companies were approaching the Chinese marketplace, how demand for various products might ebb and flow in the future, and more.

Through this process, we identified 17 specific risks across the four scan categories. And then, with those laid out in front of us, we began to rank the likelihood of each one—to assess how, if one thing changed, that might impact other risks. By creating this risk register, the client was able to begin thoughtfully adjusting their strategy with more confidence in their understanding of the underlying political risk landscape. And that, in the end, is the goal of any geostrategic scan.

THE FUTURE OF SCAN

In the coming years, as scan becomes more powerful in determining corporate success, the tools companies employ to collect, understand, and analyze changes across the globe will likely become more insightful. Already, executives and scanners have at their disposal a whole range of potential strategies for improving geostrategic competence. Some companies may want to outsource the scan function in its entirety. Others will want to develop their own teams and then braid in the perspectives that external voices can uniquely provide. The right path forward will vary from company to company and sector to sector. But every firm will likely need to find ways to improve their understanding of how the world is evolving.

For many companies, efforts to improve scan will begin on the qualitative side. They'll want to find ways to glean better analysis both from secondary research and from real people on the ground in foreign markets—people dispatched to attend various events, keep a finger on the pulse of current news and analysis, and spot emerging risks. But maintaining a sufficient, robust network can quickly drain the capacity of any given company's geostrategic team. Fortunately, the market for this sort of intelligence has spawned firms that provide high-quality information, tailored to any given company's footprint.

But that's not all that lies ahead. After years of development, new quantitative tools are also coming online. Statisticians, political scientists, and others are building sophisticated models capable of identifying political risks and opportunities that might not be unearthed by more traditional scan methods. For example, some geostrategists have built machine learning and AI algorithms to read political risk news and analysis from dozens, or even hundreds, of sources around the world to create real-time, forward-looking political risk likelihood assessments. In some cases, these models are paired with quantitative or qualitative structural analysis of political risk in a country. Such models address both sides of the Volcano Dilemma—providing both an assessment of the underlying propensity for political risk events and the near-term likelihood of their occurrence.

Other new quantitative tools use geolocation tagging. For instance, researchers at the Wharton School at the University of Pennsylvania have developed the Business and Conflict Barometer (BCB), which aggregates and analyzes thousands of geo-tagged and time-stamped qualitative and quantitative data sources. The BCB is a mixed qualitative and quantitative tool. The qualitative portion relies on deep learning, machine learning, and other natural language processing techniques. The quantitative portion depends on relational databases. Blending the two data sources enables the BCB to combine inputs from across different geographic and temporal units of analysis. In doing so, it sits at the frontier of a new field poised to lower the barriers for interested parties to explore and gain understanding of the dynamics that prevail in different global markets.

The BCB aims to help companies answer the sorts of questions that loom large ahead of major decisions. How high or low are conflict pressures related to private sector activities, and are they rising or falling for a particular project, place, region, or sector? What are the characteristics that make a specific sector prone to more or less conflict, and how do different local or country conditions affect this? How does an anticipated investment context compare to others? In any given context, what actions or initiatives distinguish less conflict-prone private sector development from that which is more so?[28]

For instance, because conflict sentiment is a leading indicator of increasing conflict, this tool can help executives better identify the societal political risks associated with a specific operational location. The BCB can thus enable executives to make better-informed decisions when considering how and where to expand into new markets. It can help geostrategists to better understand the range of risks—environmental, sociopolitical, project-specific, or actor-specific—through multivariate analyses across comparable projects and contexts. And—looking ahead to subsequent chapters—the BCB can help companies identify short-term risk *mitigation* measures and long-term risk *management* activities that can enable a more peace-positive presence within a community.

When combined with the robust qualitative reporting companies will need to do across the four categories listed above, these and other new quantitative methodologies and metrics promise to help incorporate political risk scanning into risk management systems and other quantitative structures across a company. The key here, as in the rest of scan, is to develop a range of sources and a variety of methodological approaches to reduce the likelihood that an executive will be confronted by a risk they had not anticipated or an opportunity they had not considered. No scan will ever provide certainty of a given outcome. But scan can and should provide the foundation for a much more accurate reading of the world.

However, simply identifying political risks isn't sufficient. A company needs to assess how such risks could impact their particular business. So that's where we'll turn next, pointing the way for executives to understand how the risks that have been identified could impact their company.

2

FOCUS

Assess how these political risks could affect your company

When the UK's then prime minister David Cameron first supported a referendum to give the British people an opportunity to pull the United Kingdom out of the European Union in 2013, few analysts seriously predicted that Brexit would come to be.[29] After decades of European integration, and because no European Member State had ever left the EU, it was difficult for international observers to imagine the British electorate would choose to leave—even though polls clearly indicated it was a real possibility.

Moreover, Brexit's implications *outside* of the UK and the EU were almost entirely ignored. What did it matter to an accountant in Chicago if it was harder for residents of Manchester to purchase French-made cheese? What difference would it make to a Japanese agribusiness firm if London hotels were left without the ability to hire Polish workers? Why should a Singaporean firm care if it was now going to be harder for a UK-based training provider to deliver a seminar to clients in Paris? In these and many other cases, Brexit appeared unlikely to have any noticeable business impact. So, there seemed little reason to pay much attention to the global implications.

It was only when the British did vote for Brexit, in 2016, that businesses outside of the UK began to try to understand the potential implications that would apply to them. And when the referendum was closely followed by Donald Trump's victory in America's 2016 presidential election, it prompted many to wonder whether the rise of populism and nationalism marked a broader trend toward deconstructing decades-old institutions. But if that was the "big think" concern, more "micro" consequences quickly came into clearer view. Firms that hadn't realized that their businesses were tied in a host of ways to the relationship between the UK and the EU began to feel the impacts of the coming break in those ties. And many of those firms, having failed to prepare, were left on the back foot.

Once it started to become clear how Brexit would actually be implemented—perhaps most importantly that the UK would leave the EU's single market—some of the implications were easily understood by businesses. The companies facing first-tier impacts were, in the main, aware of what they would face upon Brexit implementation. Questions, for example, of how many fish the UK and the EU could harvest in various bodies of water were sure to impact the fishing industry. And if you were a pharmaceutical company shipping medicines to hospitals and clinics in Ireland, you knew that Northern Ireland's accessibility from the Republic of Ireland—as the latter remained within the EU—was going to be complicated by the UK's exit.

But the second- and third-tier effects required more rigorous analysis to predict—on both the downside and the upside. For decades, for example, the City of London had marketed itself as a financial gateway to Europe. If a Vietnamese industrial conglomerate had wanted to finance the construction of a new mill on the outskirts of Hanoi, it might have sought out a British bank capable of leveraging interested capital from across Europe. Among the globe's financial centers, British financiers had the competitive advantage of being positioned to pull together French, Dutch, German, and other European investors eager to fund the new Vietnamese mill with minimal complication.

With Brexit, however, London's advantage started to erode—the transfer of capital from the EU to London was no longer so seamless. And that meant that financial services that might once have been provided by British firms, or, at least, by the British offices of international firms, were opened to competition. Whole books of business—often very lucrative business—were newly competitive for firms located elsewhere around the world. And the question, in many cases, was who among those firms were equipped to take advantage of that opportunity.

It was not surprising to observers that financial centers within the EU (e.g., Frankfurt, Amsterdam, and Paris) did well during this period as they maintained the access to continental assets that London could no longer seamlessly access. But, in a surprise to many analysts, the City of London remained quite robust, and American exports of financial services to the rest of the world grew by more than one-fifth. This level of growth broadly outpaced typical growth for the industry, which had averaged at less than 10 percent per year between 2004 and 2019.[30] A whole host of shifts surely played a role in driving that voracious growth. But Brexit's ripple impact was unmistakable: a British referendum proved a boon to financial firms across the Atlantic.

Brexit also provided upside opportunities to some sectors within the UK. The UK gained the ability to deviate from EU standards, which was attractive in sectors in which the UK is closer aligned with other regions of the world. A good example is insurance, in which the UK has closer ties with the US than with the EU. In 2022, the US confirmed its position as the top foreign investor in UK financial services.[31] Moreover, the US accounted for 47 percent of Lloyds of London's premium income in 2021, and this figure has been on the rise for the past decade—a trend that was uninterrupted by Brexit.[32] And total insurance premiums in the UK grew by 17 percent in 2021, a much higher figure than the annual growth average of 6 percent during the five years preceding Brexit.[33]

These diverse business impacts from a single political risk event provide a clear illustration of why companies can't stop geostrategy in scan. It's not enough to understand how the world is likely to evolve—you need to be able to anticipate how those changes will affect your business. While it was relatively clear that EU financial centers would gain new business as a result of Brexit, the dramatic shift in American banks' opportunities in the post-Brexit environment had been underappreciated. And while those arguing in favor of Brexit pointed to lower regulatory requirements as a benefit of leaving the EU, the insurance industry had not been identified as a key beneficiary.

Important business decisions—where to build relationships, how to hire appropriate professionals, how to coalesce the right teams, where to locate new facilities, and how to track down the necessary leads—required a strategic pivot. The real advantage wasn't simply in anticipating Brexit's passage, but in getting a head start capitalizing on new business opportunities born from its implementation. In competitive industries, early detection can be the difference between success and failure.

That's where "focus" comes in. Firms need to be able to determine which of the political risks they identified in scan might have a real impact, in terms of both new challenges and new opportunities. *That* task—one which requires an understanding of both how politics and policies are changing *and* how a company's business operates—marks perhaps the most difficult part of any comprehensive geostrategic process. And, as with scan, we have found that getting focus right requires a methodical and professional process.

THE IMPERATIVE OF FOCUS

The common adage is that hindsight is 20/20—that once events have unfolded, cause and effect can appear historically inevitable. And that certainly applies in the case of Brexit. But, in many cases, it's often quite difficult before the fact to identify how geostrategic shifts will impact a single industry, let alone a single company. It's a bit like dropping a pebble into a pond and anticipating how the ripples of water will impact a fish swimming on the other side. Any number of things could happen that could affect that impact. The ripple could combine with other ripples to create a large wave that the fish must navigate. Or the fish could swim to a different part of the pond before the ripple makes its impact, meaning it had no effect whatsoever.

The sense that any attempt to predict the future is futile has led some executives to simply choose *not* to invest in figuring out how various political and policy shifts might impact their own operations. We believe that's a mistake for three reasons. First, while it may not be possible to predict the impact of a pebble in the pond, a boulder that drops into it would have a more discernible impact. If an underground chemical tank began leaking into the water, the impact on that fish might be more predictable. In the same way, a war between two countries with large economies would have clear business implications for companies around the world. Many political risks have ripple effects as big as a boulder in a pond, and it's a mistake to give up on any effort to understand these future possibilities.

But even for political risks that are pebble-sized, there is value in analyzing their potential impact. These pebbles may combine with other political risks—or, indeed, with other changes in the company's external environment—that create larger waves of impact. The political risks identified in scan could be inputs into a larger sensitivity analysis to explore how different independent variables—such as a regulatory change, an economic downturn, and a shift in consumer preferences—could affect a specific dependent variable such as a company's revenue in the coming year.

Second, and perhaps more importantly, it is imperative for geostrategists to analyze and articulate the potential impacts of political risks on specific aspects of the company because that is the only way to affect how business decisions are made. So long as political risk analysis is confined to scan, it won't get the attention of the C-suite, strategy teams, and other key decision-makers. If it only summarizes political risk impacts ex post, it won't get ex ante strategic or budget focus. Focusing is, in very real terms, the only way to get the C-suite and the board to take political risk seriously.

Third, the business world is quickly developing the capability to think through just these sorts of complicated issues. Some new strategies are moored in efforts to interpret quantitative data or algorithms that illuminate a company's specific challenges and opportunities from political risks. Others apply experience and judgment to a systematically qualitative process of mapping the impact of geopolitical shifts onto various elements of an enterprise's operations. But while no system is foolproof—no process is capable of providing the same sort of 20/20 vision that seems so apparent in the aftermath of a vast change—doing focus right can give a company a competitive advantage.

The increasing strategic importance of focus is apparent in the data. EY research shows that global executives grasp the importance of assessing the impact of political risk; in fact, they prioritize it as the single most important improvement to their companies' geostrategy. The majority of executives (58 percent) identified the need for enhancements in this area—an emphasis that held across all geographies and sectors.[34] The desire for improvement is driven by a growing realization within many C-suites that the processes companies presently use to assess political risk impacts are too frequently ad hoc. The lack of more proactive impact assessments was likely part of the reason that 94 percent of executives recently reported experiencing unexpected political risk impacts in the previous year.[35] And the solution to that challenge isn't simply to improve a company's ability to understand the global landscape as it evolves. Rather, executives and board members need to craft regularized and professionalized processes for their teams to focus on how the risks identified in scan will impact their company in specific and measurable ways.

THE GROWING NEED FOR FOCUS

As discussed in the previous chapter, geopolitics has been increasingly volatile in recent years, with US-China tensions and the rising assertiveness of a variety of geopolitical swing states driving a shift from a unipolar to a multipolar world. Rising populism and nationalism have also weakened multilateral institutions as governments have exerted more control over their economies. These trends were accelerated by the COVID-19 pandemic—and then they were supercharged by the war in Ukraine. The result has been to enhance demand for focus—and to create new incentives for companies to regularize and professionalize the process. At the root is a new international trend toward national self-sufficiency. Governments around the world are becoming increasingly intent on making their economies less reliant on other countries—particularly their dependence on strategic rivals in critical sectors. As a result, governments are de-risking their economies by pursuing self-sufficiency through a variety of incentives and restrictions—with an emphasis on strategic sectors, particularly digital technologies and value chains associated with the energy transition.

Governments are using a variety of tools to achieve these goals: greater scrutiny of foreign investment; higher tariffs on international trade; export controls; subsidies and tax credits for domestic production; and other industrial policy measures. In some instances, self-sufficiency is defined more broadly to include allies and partners, with policies that promote nearshoring and friendshoring. This is a recognition both of natural resource endowments and that sourcing from allies addresses most national security concerns while limiting the trade-off with economic efficiency. These initiatives tend to be sector specific with an emphasis on strategic industries. In recent years, this geopolitical competition surrounding economic self-sufficiency has prioritized de-risking in critical technologies, such as 5G wireless networks, semiconductors, EV batteries, and AI.

Professionalized scans will reveal to many executives that the level of risk and opportunity across the globe is on the upswing—as discussed in the previous chapter. If that's the scan of the political environment, what's the focus? The political risks associated with that shift in economic policy will have impacts for companies across sectors and, within companies, across a variety of business units and functions. Focus will help C-suites take greater notice of how their *own business* is likely to change—or how it *should* change—as a result.

Supply chains and operations mark the first-order impact area for many companies and therefore provide the most obvious examples of where focus might provide important insights. Companies' production locations and supplier relationships will shift as governments restrict trade flows with geopolitical competitors and incentivize domestic production. This operational impact will be particularly significant for producers of critical or strategic products, such as semiconductors. This, in turn, will affect the supply chains across a range of sectors that purchase semiconductors. Manufacturers of automobiles, consumer electronics, and data storage providers fall into this category. And it will heighten demand for raw materials and construction services in markets that seek to provide new sources of supply. Procurement and supply chain teams will be at the forefront of shifts made to meet self-sufficiency and de-risking sourcing pressures.

Governments will also continue to impose new supply chain regulations to address heightened attention to climate change mitigation and forced labor concerns. The most notable will be the EU's proposal on corporate due diligence and accountability, which aims to encourage companies to address human rights and environmental issues throughout their entire supply chains.[36] As with other EU regulations, this is likely to have effects far beyond the EU's borders. Compliance costs will increase as firms are compelled to demonstrate their adherence to specific ESG sourcing rules—as well as to qualify for local production incentives or to address market access restrictions. Many companies are likely to need to enhance their **compliance and reporting processes** to adapt to this new geostrategic environment, in which they will likely face national security restrictions and divergent ESG regulations across different markets.

Companies' responses could create reputational risks, with win-win situations becoming increasingly difficult to find.

As more limitations on, and disincentives for, **cross-border investment** are introduced, companies are likely to have fewer cross-border M&A or investment opportunities, particularly between China and the US or EU. Technology firms are likely to find cross-border investments particularly challenging. The proliferation of trade and investment restrictions for technology and data is likely to trickle down to curtail investment opportunities for suppliers and manufacturers as well, especially those requiring strategic technologies to innovate. But these companies may, at the same time, discover new growth and investment opportunities within their home markets and in a variety of markets that are "friendly" with their home country's government. There remains significant uncertainty surrounding the future breadth and depth of these de-risking policies, though, so companies in other sectors may also be impacted.

These geostrategic shifts will ripple through other areas of companies as well. **Talent** in certain locations will be at an ever-higher premium as reshoring continues and various labor markets remain tight. At the same time, companies' approaches to ESG issues are likely to remain a differentiator in attracting and retaining talent, particularly among younger employees. And government approaches to ESG will affect companies' strategies for where they employ workers globally.

At a macro level, these policies are likely to weigh on economic growth and stoke inflation because diminished cross-border trade and investment will reduce economic

efficiency. The likely shift to higher-cost suppliers and producers could heighten companies' input costs across sectors
and geographies. These inflationary impacts also raise the
cost of capital. Elevated interest rates may make it harder
for some companies to obtain credit and meet existing debt
obligations. However, this could present opportunities for
private equity firms and nontraditional lenders. The financial sector is likely to have opportunities to accrue higher
revenues, even as they face the risks born from nonperform-
ing loans and defaults.

As governments' cost of borrowing increases, they will
feel compelled in some cases to raise **taxes**, particularly in
emerging markets. Food and fuel subsidies may be reduced or
removed in some markets, which will add to the cost of doing
business. Some governments may also raise taxes on companies, particularly in high-growth sectors, in order to finance
industrial policies and social programs. For instance, high
commodity prices, when combined with the energy transition, will elevate demand for green metals and minerals.
Governments may react by imposing windfall or profit taxes,
or higher duties and excise rates, on mining companies.

Companies are likely to face stricter regulation of digital
technologies, with the EU and China continuing to be leaders in this space. **Data privacy and data security** will be key
tools in regulators' toolboxes, particularly in Asia. Taken in
tandem, the proliferation of data localization and data privacy rules will make moving or sharing data across borders
more difficult. Financial services, e-commerce firms, digital service providers, and industrial equipment manufacturers are likely to be affected most acutely. The extractive

industries, which operate in areas considered to be politically sensitive by host governments, may also be subject to new data localization requirements. Certain companies, including those in the technology sector and those engaging in M&A transactions, will likely be at heightened risk of cyberattacks. Software providers may be in the crosshairs, as they offer hackers a means of distributing malware to a wide range of organizations.

Finally, geopolitical tensions and government policies that effectively restrict the size of a company's global market will change **sales and revenue** projections. The competition that companies face is likely to shift; although a company's core competitor might have previously been located in a geopolitical rival's market, now new competition may emerge through the friendshoring trend. And if geopolitical tensions worsen, the global economy will face trade barriers and elevated conflict, which will inevitably constrain revenue growth opportunities. And, at a country level, if governments are unable to address incomes being squeezed by high inflation and the cost of credit, sales and revenue growth are likely to be depressed. But companies with lower-cost products could benefit as consumers shift toward more affordable brands and product categories.

THE BENEFITS OF FOCUS

What has become increasingly clear in recent years is that even companies that believe they're largely insulated from changes in the geopolitical realm are, in practice, deeply intertwined. For example, executives might presume that political efforts aimed at reducing their home country's dependence on its trade partners do not impact them, because the company's suppliers and customers are overwhelmingly domestic. But cursory looks often miss the second- and third-order implications. That firm might not be sourcing from a foreign company, but its suppliers may be entirely dependent on imports. That firm might not be selling to a foreign market, but its customers may be dependent on income earned abroad. In other words, even businesses that *appear* to be set apart from geopolitical concerns are often deeply integrated. So, their executives need to pay close attention to the wider world.

We're already seeing clear benefits for companies that use scan and focus. For example, a company with a diversified supply chain, drawing parts and labor from across Central and Eastern Europe, worried as tensions ratcheted up between Ukraine and Russia. The question for the company's executives wasn't whether they would or would not be vulnerable—they knew they were. Rather, the question was where and how they were vulnerable, and how they could mitigate any likely business disruptions—in essence, the question was regarding how to prioritize their vulnerabilities.

So, when Moscow mobilized against Kyiv in early 2022, executives quickly moved forward with a focus assessment of how their company could be impacted if the war escalated or spread to other geographies. Their immediate challenge was to determine where they were most vulnerable so that they could pivot more quickly to find alternatives. What could they source from farther away? How would they get supplies and parts expeditiously to their plants in Europe? What was likely to remain available locally? How would their workers be impacted? What raw materials did they actually have in their production process, and how would they be impacted? And how could they prepare themselves to respond to a variety of second- and third-tier shifts that might emerge depending on the evolution of the war?

For instance, they prepared for the possibility that the Russian offensive might reach beyond Ukraine or that energy supplies to the regions where their suppliers had factories could be cut off. They did so by identifying and setting up monitoring for a series of signposts that would likely signal an escalation of tensions in the conflict that could lead to greater impact on their supply chain. These efforts to engage in scan and focus ensured that they would not be caught flat-footed in the future.

Here, again, what's clear is that the key to dealing with political risk centers not just on understanding what might happen in the world, but on understanding how any individual firm or industry's strengths and vulnerabilities line up against those potential changes. Perhaps a company sources some of its raw materials from several different suppliers, presuming that those suppliers are gathering the underlying materials from a range of different countries. If, in fact, all of its suppliers are actually harvesting materials from the same place, then a single disruption—if, for example, exports are cut off because of a civil war—will reveal an unseen vulnerability. By failing to know the original source of the materials, executives would have assumed the company was more resilient than it really was.

Or suppose a company is selling its goods to a range of buyers, but all of those buyers are then selling the goods to the same small market of consumers. If there's a sudden disruption in that market—if a recession hits and individuals living there are no longer equipped to continue purchasing the company's goods—then the company is similarly vulnerable. In *both* cases, political risk is hidden by a company's failure to see beyond its arms-length contacts. Executives may *think* that they've diversified their supply chain or their consumer market—but, in fact, they are almost as vulnerable as they would have been if they had come to depend on a single supplier or had to sell their products to one sliver of a single market.

In some cases, there may be no alternative. Certain defense contractors, for example, view their market as a single military command. But many companies can mitigate risk by taking a more professionalized approach to focus. Fortunately, new technology is now available to aggregate and analyze data such that executives can glean a much clearer picture of what's *really* happening. One such tool, developed by EY teams, is called the Business Relationship Economic Threat Analysis (BRETA).[37]

EY BRETA serves as an analytics platform to analyze and identify multidimensional risks facing companies and their connected parties, providing insights on the geopolitical, country, regulatory, and societal political risks associated with the countries in which companies—and their suppliers—are doing business. And it has already proven invaluable to several EY clients.

In the immediate wake of the Russian invasion of Ukraine in 2022, for example, the magnitude of companies' responses was mixed. Many executives believed that their companies had full visibility into the risks they faced and were therefore managing them appropriately. However, as the impacts spread—primarily via supply chains and in financial services—new risks and complexities arose. Executives realized they needed to better understand their current exposure via enhanced data analytics, active monitoring, due diligence, and other investigative measures to find all affected current business relationships—no matter how obscure.

EY BRETA provided these much-needed answers, particularly around sanctions compliance. Multiple teams were involved in collecting, compiling, and validating lists of sanctioned entities and individuals. Then, starting from an individual company, a multinodal ecosystem network could be built to compare against the sanctioned entity list. This "outside-in" approach supplemented companies' own knowledge of direct relationships with a variety of indirect relationships via tier-2 and tier-3 suppliers. Unsurprisingly, companies in the energy sector were most at risk of sanctions noncompliance, with an average of 20 tier-2 and 301 tier-3 suppliers identified. This amounted to almost US$137 billion in revenue at risk.

HOW TO FOCUS

The previous chapter outlined a leading process for identifying potential geostrategic changes—that is, for scan. But simply pulling together a list isn't enough to prepare for potential risks and opportunities. Executives need also to understand how shifts in the political landscape are likely to affect their business *specifically*. To do that, they must be able to map the impact of political risks across a full panoply of their company's functions and business units or geographies (see figure 4).

Focus may well be the most difficult aspect of geostrategy. It demands both systematic consideration and imagination. It requires a geostrategist both to understand how the world is evolving *and* how their own company operates across a whole range of functions. But, if professionalized, it can be done well. And focus done well can open doors for companies that would otherwise have remained unseen.

In order to focus, the geostrategy team must first analyze how the company operates. There is, of course, no one-size-fits-all template for disaggregating the elements of every firm's operations. But, generally speaking, we find that these seven functions are broadly applicable across

FIGURE 4.
FOCUS: ASSESS THE IMPACT OF POLITICAL RISKS ON COMPANY FUNCTIONS AND THE GLOBAL FOOTPRINT

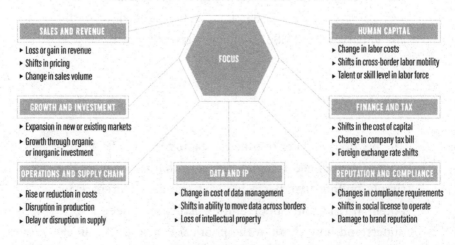

SALES AND REVENUE
- Loss or gain in revenue
- Shifts in pricing
- Change in sales volume

FOCUS

HUMAN CAPITAL
- Change in labor costs
- Shifts in cross-border labor mobility
- Talent or skill level in labor force

GROWTH AND INVESTMENT
- Expansion in new or existing markets
- Growth through organic or inorganic investment

FINANCE AND TAX
- Shifts in the cost of capital
- Change in company tax bill
- Foreign exchange rate shifts

OPERATIONS AND SUPPLY CHAIN
- Rise or reduction in costs
- Disruption in production
- Delay or disruption in supply

DATA AND IP
- Change in cost of data management
- Shifts in ability to move data across borders
- Loss of intellectual property

REPUTATION AND COMPLIANCE
- Changes in compliance requirements
- Shifts in social license to operate
- Damage to brand reputation

Source: EY Geostrategic Business Group.

companies: sales and revenue; growth and investment; operations and supply chain; data and intellectual property (IP); human capital; finance and tax; and reputation and compliance. Depending on a company's size, complexity, and geographic footprint, executives may also assess political risk impacts across country or regional divisions and across business units.

For instance, in the immediate wake of the beginning of the war in Ukraine in 2022, many executives sought to understand how the conflict could impact their company. There was a deluge of news stories on the war and on the resulting government policy responses. The result was that it was often hard to get a handle on the scan—let alone the focus—aspect of geostrategy. Executives needed an impact analysis template to both structure the political risks that were arising and assess the impacts of a variety of key disruption vectors (see figure 5). Such an impact analysis effort cannot only enable the geostrategy team to conduct more structured analyses, but should also better articulate why other teams, functions, and business units should care.

It is also important to identify or invest in political risk impact assessments at the functional or business unit levels. Companies that excel at focus leverage the capabilities of their leaders at the functional, business unit, or country levels—not just the core geostrategy team level—to manage political risks. Companies that build or operationalize this capacity will understand the specific pathways by which political risks affect their company—as well as how they can act at the business unit or country level to influence the political risks they face. This enables companies to embed

FIGURE 5.
ILLUSTRATIVE FRAMEWORK FOR CONSIDERATION OF COMPANY IMPACTS FROM THE WAR IN UKRAINE

Source of disruption	Disruption vectors	Illustrative business impact by function						
		Sales and revenue	Growth and investment	Operations and supply chain	Data and IP	Human capital	Finance and tax	Reputation and compliance
Immediate security issues	• Physical threats to the safety and well-being of employees and their families • Physical threats to the security of equipment and stocks							
Financial sanctions	• Sanctions on financial and corporate sectors • Targeted sanctions on individuals and their assets • Sanctions on central banks							
Export and capital controls	• Formal export controls on goods or components, including with third countries • Capital controls and restrictions on withdrawals, transfers, and securities sales, etc.							
General business disruptions	• Investment restrictions and forced disinvestment • State-mandated operational restrictions (e.g., payment systems) • Infrastructure disruption in local area and global closures of specific businesses (e.g., airspace, ports, oil and gas pipelines, utilities) • Displacement of consumers and employees (e.g., voluntary evacuation, refugee flows)							

Private sector and civil society	• Permanent and temporary business responses
	   • Corporate-driven disinvestment and operational closures, including on internet platforms
	   • Supplier responses (e.g., re-prioritization of supplies)
	   • Competitors restricting sales in affected countries leading to consumer pressure
	• Customer and employee responses (e.g., boycotts, social activism)
	• Market competition from non-sanction or export control implementing countries							

Cyber	• Direct cyberattacks on individual businesses and organizations (state- and non-state-sponsored) • Cyberattacks on critical and digital infrastructure (e.g., energy, internet or telecoms, government facilities, satellite systems) • Closure of B2C channels, including social media platforms							
Markets and macroeconomy	• Market volatility and impacts (including interest rate, inflation, GDP growth, foreign exchange) • Energy market disruptions and price volatility • Raw material market disruptions and price volatility • Reduced consumer confidence							

Executives should consider assessing impact on industry, sector, or individual company footprint. A possible impact assessment scale could be:

High   Medium   Low or N/A

EY Geostrategic Business Group.

74

political risk assessments into their daily operations and strategic plans in the functions, geographies, or business units where political risk impact is the highest. For those areas where political risk is most material, leaders should be conscientious about integrating political risk assessments into operations and strategy—a point we'll explore in more detail in later chapters.

Each function or business unit comprises a range of its own idiosyncrasies. Various elements of a company's business endeavors will be more vulnerable to certain geostrategic shifts, meaning that executives with responsibility for that particular function will need to pay particular attention. The different functions will respond to different circumstances in disparate ways across companies and sectors. That's why having a structure to focus is so important. Gleaning real wisdom from geostrategy requires a thoughtful analysis of how changes will filter through any company's range of functions. Below are some academic research and real-world examples illustrating how companies can be impacted by political risk across the seven functions we typically assess, and some questions that geostrategists can ask to assess the likely impact of a potential political risk on their company.

SALES AND REVENUE

In the *Geostrategy in Practice 2021* study, 70 percent of global executives said political risk events had had a high impact on their company's revenue in the previous year.[38] Companies can face a political risk of losing sales to customers who are looking to reduce purchases due to the national origin or reputation of the seller, or to those who are averse to paying higher prices that result from government policies (e.g., tariffs, quotas, or regulations). For instance, a multinational company's sales are likely to be impacted if a wave of nationalism sweeps across a country's consumer market, or if a change in government prompts the imposition of a drastic new tariff.

One example of trade policy shifts affecting companies' revenue is a US-EU trade dispute that led to the EU imposing higher tariffs on American whiskey imports in June 2018. The Distilled Spirits Council of the United States estimates that US whiskey exports to the EU dropped 20 percent during the imposition of these tariffs—which were suspended in January 2022—representing a loss of hundreds of millions of US dollars in revenue for the affected companies.[39]

Companies need to pay particularly close attention to geopolitical risks to consumer tastes and preferences where their sales are focused. During the US-led Iraq War in the early 2000s, for example, American companies saw sales decline throughout the Middle East, with US sales growth lagging foreign competition by 21 percent from 2002 to 2003. And, during the period of contentious debt negotiations between Greece and the EU—in which the German government took a tough stance—German auto sales dropped 15 percent in Greece over a 12-month period.[40] These are clear examples of how a seemingly unrelated geopolitical shift can impact sales and revenue in profound ways.

To focus on the potential revenue impacts of a political risk on their company, geostrategists can ask the following questions:

- What share of the company's revenue is exposed to the political risk?

- How would the company's customers be affected? How would changes in customer or consumer demand affect revenue growth?

- Which goods' and services' sales would be affected by the political risk? How would that affect the company's product portfolio?

- How would the political risk affect the company's pricing?

- Where else could the company shift its revenue growth targets to make up for the impact from this political risk?

GROWTH AND INVESTMENT

Political risks can also affect companies' growth prospects and their investments. At the macro level, higher levels of geopolitical risk are correlated with lower corporate investment.[41] Changes in a country's political environment can have a profound impact on where a business decides to invest its resources. Military conflict in a market, for example, often leads to less investment. A study of more than 4,000 mining firms in 177 countries found that firms reduced investment by 8 percent in locales that have recently experienced a fatal armed conflict.[42] Another study found that the outbreak of violent conflict near a subsidiary increases the likelihood of divestment by 52 percent.[43]

It's not only large-scale, headline-grabbing political risks, such as wars, that affect companies' investment decisions. For instance, a study examining the locations of almost 7,000 US multinational subsidiaries indicated that a one standard deviation decrease in the quality of a country's property rights protections diminished the incidence of market entry by 1.8 percent.[44]

Recent interest in enhancing antitrust enforcement and more restrictive cross-border investment policies, such as strengthening the mandate of the Committee on Foreign Investment in the United States (CFIUS), are similarly likely to dampen cross-border M&A activity. Political risks can also affect the performance of cross-border M&As that do proceed. A study in the US revealed that multinational firms from countries with greater political affinity to the US experience significantly stronger post-acquisition performance—with up to 35 percent higher firm value three years after the acquisition.[45] More broadly, experience in a country and familiarity with the political system and its players has been found to reduce the threat of failure by 80 percent.[46] And companies from countries with higher levels of political risk have been found to be less deterred from expansion in other politically risky countries.[47]

New or newly attractive investment opportunities can also present themselves as a result of political or policy changes. For instance, Indonesia banned the export of raw nickel in 2020 in an effort to encourage foreign companies to invest in domestic processing of the material. With the rapid increase in demand for EVs, more companies see investment opportunities in Indonesia's nickel-processing industry. For instance, in 2023, South Korean steelmaker POSCO announced an investment of US$441 million to build a nickel refinery in Indonesia that will produce nickel intermediates for use in rechargeable batteries such as those in EVs.[48]

To focus on the potential growth and investment impacts of a political risk on their company, geostrategists can ask the following questions:

- How would the political risk affect organic growth prospects, including second-order effects, such as impacts on overall economic growth?

- How would the company's M&A strategy be affected?

- Would the political risk limit growth or investment opportunities in certain geographies or market segments?

- Would the political risk expand growth or investment opportunities in any areas?

- What would be the impact, if any, on the company's corporate structure and portfolio?

OPERATIONS AND SUPPLY CHAIN

In recent years, significant geopolitical developments have dramatically changed the ways firms source material and component parts.[49] During the pandemic, supply bottlenecks and, in some cases, export restrictions exacerbated supply chain pressures on companies that operate across borders. In extreme cases, countries even erected physical barriers to trade. One study found such barriers were, on average, associated with a 31 percent reduction in bilateral trade.[50]

In a recent survey, 92 percent of global executives expected political risks to have the greatest impact on their company's operations and supply chain.[51] In another survey, 41 percent of executives said that geopolitical challenges have prompted their companies to reconfigure their supply chains—with restrictive regulatory, trade, and investment policies as the most common drivers of that decision.[52] However, rising geopolitical tensions are more likely to affect some companies more than others. A study on the bilateral trade patterns of China and India found that political tensions impacted the imports of state-owned enterprise (SOE) more than those of private companies.[53]

There are a variety of recent examples of supply chain shifts that have been motivated at least in part by political risks. In recent years, for instance, US-based footwear producer Crocs had proactively diversified its supply chains from China to Vietnam. Then, in the summer of 2021, Vietnam's strict COVID-19 restrictions led Crocs to move some production to Indonesia and to Bosnia and Herzegovina. The company is embracing diversification in its supply chain, having opened a second factory in Indonesia and expanding to India.[54] In another example, the Denmark-based wind turbine manufacturer Vestas built two new factories in India, in 2021, to capitalize on the country's rapidly expanding renewables market and to diversify its supply chains, in response to the impact of China's zero-COVID-19 policy.[55]

Free trade agreements are important to consider when evaluating how political risks affect companies' global supply chains. New trade agreements can shift the cost and regulatory compliance associated with sourcing from different countries. As just one example, consider how the Comprehensive and Progressive Agreement for Trans-Pacific Partnership (CPTPP) facilitated cross-border flows between two of its initial ratifying members. In the first six months after the CPTPP went into force on December 30, 2018, Japanese imports of goods from Vietnam jumped 7 percent.[56] Compare that to how Japan's overall imports over the same period fell by 1.1 percent.[57] Perhaps even more significantly, Japanese exports to Vietnam have grown significantly since the CPTPP entered into force.[58] Many analysts attribute this growth to the CPTPP's facilitation of e-commerce as well as the commitments Vietnam made to reduce regulations for foreign retailers.[59] And, in a 2022 survey of Japanese businesses, Vietnam ranked second globally in terms of countries in which they planned to expand their overseas business—the highest rank for any Southeast Asian country.[60]

To focus on the potential operations and supply chain impacts of a political risk on their company, geostrategists can ask these questions:

- How would the political risk affect operating costs for the company?

- Would the political risk cause any disruptions or delays at the company's production locations? Are alternative production locations available?

- Would it cause any disruptions or delays at the company's suppliers? If so, which ones, and how concentrated or critical are those suppliers to the company's operations?

- How would the political risk affect the operating model and supply chain strategy for the company (e.g., onshoring, nearshoring, and friendshoring)?

- What effect would these operations and supply chain impacts have on top-line and bottom-line performance?

DATA AND INTELLECTUAL PROPERTY

Political risk can affect data, R&D, and IP rights in a variety of ways. Those impacts will only become more profound as new digital technologies, such as 5G wireless networks and generative AI—and the data that they generate and use— become more pervasive. This is likely to be particularly true in countries with high levels of political risk, where corporations face the threat of IP theft and the potential loss of market share to domestic competitors. Companies that are technology leaders were, in one study, eight times more sensitive to political risk than their technologically lagging counterparts.[61]

Companies' data management systems are also increasingly affected by the proliferation of regulations surrounding data security and data privacy in key markets, which will continue to increase data-sharing costs across borders. Multinational companies that handle data extensively, particularly personal or consumer data, and those that use third-party service providers, such as cloud services or data storage, are likely to be most affected by these regulations. One notable example is the EU's GDPR, which went into effect in 2018. It was the first significant data privacy policy in a major market, and it has influenced how companies around the world manage personal data. Just one example of its effect on business decisions was seen in 2020, when Microsoft announced a US$1.5 billion investment in Italy that included the company's first data center in the country, which will enable compliance with the GDPR.[62]

In terms of R&D, many governments rely on tax and other incentives to promote investment and innovation within their economies. One such example is observable in Brazil, where the government established the Brazilian Company of Research and Industrial Innovation (EMBRAPII) in 2013 to facilitate collaboration among technological research institutions and industrial companies and to promote innovation. While this can include both financial and nonfinancial support, the financial contribution is limited to 33 percent of the total amount of the R&D project. In the first 10 years of its existence, EMBRAPII supported more than 1,400 companies, leading to approximately 660 intellectual property requests.[63]

To focus on the potential data and intellectual property impacts of a political risk on their company, geostrategists can ask these questions:

- How would the political risk affect data management costs for the company?
- Would the political risk affect how the company analyzes and monetizes data?
- Would the company's intellectual property rights be affected?
- How would the political risk affect the company's cross-border sharing of technology, customer data, and other intellectual property?
- Does the political risk change the company's exposure to cyberattacks?

HUMAN CAPITAL

If immigration rules change, if visa requirements shift, or if travel flows are disrupted, a company may lose access to some of its staff and advisors. There is also evidence that changes in visa policies affect the availability of talent in the target market. A recent study examined the effects of two different policy changes that restricted access to US H1-B visas—which are designated primarily for immigrants with a bachelor's degree who work in a "specialty occupation." The impact on many companies was a shift of their human capital footprint for those occupations to other markets such as China, India, and Canada.[64] Immigration policies can also affect other parts of the talent value chain, including at academic institutions in terms of both international students and researchers.

Firms exposed to political risk also tend to retrench hiring activities. One study found that a single standard deviation increase in political risk was associated with an 11.5 percent decrease in employment growth compared to the average company.[65] Policy changes can also lead to shifts in talent management. For instance, the German Association of the Automotive Industry has estimated that at least 215,000 jobs in their industry will be affected by energy transition regulations.[66] To manage this shift, some companies have already announced significant reskilling programs for current employees.

Most dramatically, domestic and civil conflict present a physical threat to companies and their workforces, to which companies respond with interventions ranging from private security to negotiations to peace-building.[67, 68] As many companies have experienced firsthand in recent years, international conflict also poses human capital impacts. When Russia invaded Ukraine, many companies with Russian units were forced to choose between maintaining their operations in Russia—a decision that created serious reputational risk in the West—or terminating their Russian employees (including, potentially, through selling their assets in Russia). And firms with units in Ukraine mobilized, in many cases, to relocate their employees to safety, incurring substantial cost but retaining their talent.

To focus on the potential human capital impacts of a political risk on their company, geostrategists can ask these questions:

- How would the political risk change the company's cost of employing workers?

- Would the political risk affect cross-border labor mobility?

- How would the political risk affect the skill level of the labor force in the markets in which the company operates?

- To what extent would the company face talent shortages as a result of the political risk?

- Would the political risk affect the safety and security of the company's workforce?

FINANCE AND TAX

Economic policy uncertainty affects company finances by increasing the cost of capital. Increases in global economic policy uncertainty have been shown to increase the average weighted cost of capital at the macro level.[69] More broadly, increasing political risk at the country level from the 25th to the 75th percentile equates, approximately, to a 3 percent increase in the cost of capital.[70] Heightened levels of political risk can also affect other financial considerations for certain projects, such as the cost of political risk or trade credit insurance.

Geopolitical relations can also affect the tax rates companies face abroad. One study found that a single standard deviation decline in the strength of diplomatic relations between countries will drive up a foreign company's tax costs by 15 percent to 25 percent, on average.[71] US-China trade tensions are a case in point. The US initially imposed "Section 301" tariffs (an indirect tax) on a variety of imports from China in 2018 and 2019, resulting in higher costs for companies importing affected goods into the US from China—regardless of the nationality of those companies. Indeed, the US International Trade Commission estimates nearly all of these elevated tariff costs were borne by the importing companies.[72]

Specific events, such as elections, can also have impacts on company finances. For example, one study found uncertainty associated with a US election cycle negatively affects equity returns in foreign countries, with stronger effects when a country has larger equity market exposure to foreign investors. And while the reaction of non-US market indices was approximately –1 percent in the six-month period prior to an election, it was even greater (–2.4 percent) when there was more uncertainty in political power outcomes—such as a swing in control of either Congressional chamber.[73]

To focus on the potential finance and tax impacts of a political risk on their company, geostrategists can ask these questions:

- How would the political risk affect the company's access to capital?
- How would the company's capital allocation priorities and the capital structure shift as a result of the political risk?
- What would be the changes in the company's tax bill that result from the political risk?

- How would the political risk affect cross-border financial transfers, the use of specific international payments systems, and exchange rate risks for the company?

- Would the political risk affect the viability of the company's ownership or governance structure (e.g., joint ventures or subsidiaries)?

REPUTATION AND COMPLIANCE

In the EY *Geostrategy in Practice 2021* survey, global executives pointed to regulatory risks as the most impactful for reputation and compliance (27 percent), followed by societal risks (20 percent).[74] Changes in regulations can affect compliance costs and even companies' business models. One notable example was the aforementioned introduction of the EU's GDPR, which obliged many companies—including those that monitor data or process personal data on a large scale—to appoint a Data Protection Officer (DPO).[75] For instance, Spain's data protection authority announced in January 2023 that more than 100,000 DPOs had registered in the country.[76] In some cases, this role was assigned to an existing employee, while in others it required hiring talent with the necessary skills.

Societal risks are also impactful, particularly as civil society groups have become more prone to pressure companies using public "corporate responsibility" campaigns. Among the most widely cited examples of societal risks impacting companies' reputations are the "anti-sweatshop" campaigns targeted at apparel and footwear companies in the 1990s and 2000s. One exploration of that movement categorized how reputational impacts, in some circumstances, affected apparel and footwear companies' sales, stock prices, and the design of corporate responsibility ratings.[77] A more recent study found companies facing social boycotts experience 30 percent higher board turnover.[78] Yet, this pressure, according to one forthcoming study, differs across countries based on the political strength of civil society.[79]

It's not just concerns emanating from civil society that pose risks (upside and downside) to companies' reputations. According to the *2020 EY Climate Change and Sustainability Services (CCaSS) Institutional Investor* survey, 67 percent of investors surveyed now make "significant use" of ESG disclosures that are shaped by the Task Force on Climate-related Financial Disclosures (TCFD).[80] Multinational firms, in particular, are at relatively higher risk due to the liability of being foreign and private in association with environmental and social issues.[81, 82] One recent study on the global mining industry, for instance, found that equity markets apply a discount to announcements that indicate a company's mines are close to environmentally sensitive water resources.[83]

To focus on the potential reputation and compliance impacts of a political risk on their company, geostrategists can ask these questions:

- How would the political risk change the company's compliance costs?

- Would the political risk generate new compliance requirements or create the need for additional compliance capabilities?

- Would the political risk affect the company's brand reputation, either negatively or positively? How would this effect differ across markets?

- How would the company's stakeholder communications and reputation management strategy shift as a result of the political risk?

- How would the political risk affect the company's social license to operate in key markets?

THE ART OF FOCUS

At its core, focus is about developing, acquiring, and improving a company's ability to assess the business impact of political risk. As such, focus requires not only a firm grasp of the intelligence gleaned from scan, but also a clear picture of what's happening *inside* a given business. Focus requires not only a solid understanding of the political environment, but real business knowledge and experience as well. For geostrategy to work, this "secret sauce" of scan and focus need to blend together seamlessly. C-suite executives need to understand how political risk intersects with a company's business.

That can often prove a challenge. About one-third of companies do no better than a coin flip in terms of identifying political risk events that would impact them—that is, they were surprised by political risk impacts about half the time.[84] And while that's partially due to challenges identifying risks, executives point to improving impact assessments as their tallest hurdle. Most companies (and political risk analysts) struggle to translate how identified political risks will impact the business across specific functions and performance metrics. The focus framework and impact questions presented in this chapter provide a starting point for how to approach this analysis.

If focus is almost invariably hard to do well, it can be made more manageable if political risk impact assessments employed at the functional or business unit level are integrated with those being used within the C-suite. Everything needs to fit together so that functional and business unit impact assessments inform enterprise-wide assessments—and vice versa. Over time, the process of mapping global shifts to a company's own business function will become more process-driven, more accurate, and more powerful. It may be impossible for a company to mitigate *all* political risks—but if a firm does scan and focus well, executives will be more capable of *managing* risks over the short, medium, and long term. This is the process we'll turn to in the next chapter.

3
MANAGE

Integrate political risk into
connected risk approaches

To this point, we have explored scan, which describes the risk identification process organizations may use to gather a more comprehensive roster of the political risks—including both challenges and opportunities—that they face, and the likelihood of those risks occurring. We've also looked thoroughly at focus, examining how a company can assess the impact the various risks could have on their business. For companies seeking to equip themselves to thrive in an increasingly complex global environment, the next steps are to evaluate how those likelihoods and impacts map against each other and to determine how to actively manage them. It's only by drawing from scan and focus that a company can progress to a sophisticated approach to managing political risk (see figure 6).

Begin with the simple definition of risk. The Committee of Sponsoring Organizations of the Treadway Commission (COSO)—a leading authority on risk management, governance, and fraud deterrence—defines risk as the "possibility that events will occur and affect the achievement of strategy

FIGURE 6.
MANAGE: INTEGRATE POLITICAL RISK INTO CONNECTED RISK APPROACHES

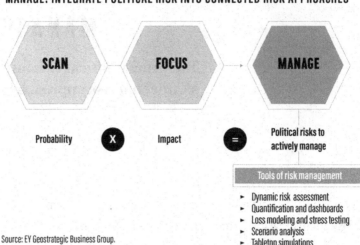

Source: EY Geostrategic Business Group.

and business objectives."[85] This, for many executives, will be familiar. Importantly, not all risks are treated the same in the corporate world. While some potential risks may be viewed as having a lower likelihood of occurrence, their impact on business strategy and objectives could be so significant that they warrant C-suite attention. Other risks may have a high likelihood but wouldn't have a material effect on the company. By the same token, managing each risk in isolation is insufficient.[86] Executives must consider how different risks may interact and possibly affect the entire enterprise—on both the upside and the downside.

Every company, of course, manages risk of one kind or another. But, as the global EY organization has found in its research, many executives worry that they don't manage risk—political or otherwise—well. The *EY Global Board Risk Survey 2023* revealed that only 40 percent of board members believed their organization is sufficiently addressing emerging risks in their risk management frameworks.[87] This suggests that the risks with the biggest increase in concern—including political risk—are also some of the most difficult to identify, assess, and manage.

That is, in part, because individual risks are often addressed as stand-alone tasks in siloed business areas, rather than being managed at the company-wide level. And so, in this context, the challenge for many companies is twofold: to begin thinking about risk in a more comprehensive way, and then to ensure that geopolitics and other political risks are woven into that broader portfolio. The sales team in Asia, for example, might be aware of how election results in a country in their region could affect the market appetite for a company's product. Alternatively, those managing a company's supply chain might understand why a heightening conflict in South America would *not* likely affect the company's ability to obtain certain raw materials because the managers know the materials could be purchased from suppliers in Africa instead. But how do these various pockets of knowledge filter up to an enterprise-wide assessment and a plan to manage these risks? In these examples, how does the C-suite gain the ability to collectively track the business consequences of any one political risk across the enterprise?

This is, by some measure, the reason that a connected risk approach, across the enterprise, has emerged as a leading practice. Some organizations pursue this approach through entrusting integrated risk responsibilities to the "enterprise risk management" function, or ERM. The "E" is important because ERM is designed to provide a top-down, enterprise view of all the significant risks that could affect the strategic objectives of an organization.[88] But, in today's world, the "E" can also stand for "ecosystem," as there is an increasing recognition that risk management must go beyond the boundaries of the enterprise to encompass a company's entire ecosystem. ERM or other connected risk approaches are designed to not only give company leaders a 30,000-foot view of *all* the risks and opportunities facing a business, but also to give decision-makers sufficient visibility to track emerging areas of risk so strategic action can be taken in a timely manner. This also empowers companies to set priorities—to put to the side less consequential concerns so that the more impactful and more likely risks get the concern and attention they deserve.

Importantly, the goal here is not simply to ensure that the operations team is aware of what the sales team already knows or that the marketing team isn't blindsided by something the finance team uncovered months earlier. The goal is to build comprehensive groupings of risk areas, with monitoring and reporting systems for each. And it is to, thereafter, begin to form the full picture of risks from across the organization, which gives decision-makers broader insight into how a change in one aspect of an organization would affect other parts of a company's strategy and operations. Executives need to know how risks will *cascade*. Perhaps a high-probability, low-impact risk appears, at first, to be of little concern. But then, through a connected risk approach, executives can consider whether one relatively minor risk would increase the likelihood of a high-impact risk in another realm of the company's operations. And, importantly, risk management isn't a "one and done" process, but it must account for the dynamic nature of risks and the different velocities with which they evolve over time.

The challenge today is to apply all of this to *political* risk, which, as we have established in our discussion of scan and focus, is too often overlooked even while becoming increasingly important. Companies' connected risk approaches need to evolve so that the same synergies that have emerged by breaking down silos in *other* areas apply to changes on the political risk front as well.

THE NEED FOR POLITICAL RISK MANAGEMENT

As we've established, political risk has risen in severity and will remain elevated as globalization continues to evolve. But even as that reality has come into clearer view, companies have been slow to incorporate political risk into their broader risk management processes. While companies that use a PESTLE or PESTEL framework for external risks—which separates risks into six categories: political, economic, social, technological, legal, and environmental—may already do this to some extent, the "P" (political) often needs to be more robust to be effective.[89] That's because political risk can be what is often termed a "strategic risk"—a challenge so fundamental that, if it manifests, it will make it difficult or even impossible for the company to achieve its business objectives and implement its strategy. In other words, strategic risks are those that can significantly affect stakeholder value and even the viability of the company in the long term.[90]

The need for improved political risk management was made clear during the recent global pandemic. The COVID-19 pandemic created an unprecedented global business environment. The virus's spread effectively halted international travel, shut down factories, and turned shopping districts into ghost towns, leaving impacts on companies in every industry and in every major market around the world. It was, first and foremost, a human tragedy. But it was *also* a public health and governance crisis driven by political risks born of export controls, industrial policies to increase "self-sufficiency" in critical products, vaccine nationalism, and vaccine diplomacy.

Whereas some of the risks brought on by the pandemic were of the sort that traditional risk management systems might have anticipated, many of the political risk elements were not. Pre-pandemic, 74 percent of global executives were highly confident about their company's ability to manage political risks. In the wake of the pandemic, only 55 percent of global executives displayed similar confidence levels.[91] That's clear evidence that executives need a more strategic approach to managing political risk. But the pandemic wasn't the first beacon. The global financial crisis of 2008 and 2009 provided early evidence of how risks that began in the banking sector could swiftly migrate into the political realm and ripple in unexpected ways across the world. And the war in Ukraine has proven the same point. Today, no one can really dispute that risk management and crisis response systems need to be honed to adapt in real time to a rapidly changing, global business environment. But, far too often, companies doing this well provide the exception to the rule.

In the *EY Global Board Risk Survey 2023*, for instance, 60 percent of boards said that emerging risks are insufficiently addressed in risk management frameworks.[92]

One example of a company demonstrating adept management of political risk comes from the pharmaceutical sector. When the US government capped the price of insulin at US$35 per month for seniors on Medicare in the Inflation Reduction Act of 2022, many pharmaceutical executives immediately realized that there would be pressure to cut prices for other insulin consumers as well.[93] Indeed, US President Biden announced in his 2023 State of the Union address that he was committed to extending this price cap. Sensing the coming market change, several C-suites saw an opportunity. US pharmaceutical company Eli Lilly, for example, announced in March 2023 that it would lower the price of its most commonly prescribed insulins by 70 percent.[94] The company was able to claim first-mover advantage in announcing the price cuts, demonstrating strategic alignment with their stakeholders, including policymakers, regulators, and customers.

But actions such as this remain the exception—most companies have been slow to integrate political risk into their risk systems. In the most recent EY *Geostrategy in Practice* survey, only 23 percent of global executives reported that their company integrates political risk management into broader risk management on a regular or proactive basis. And only 35 percent of executives said that they perform political risk management activities on a proactive or regular basis.[95] That's a problem because companies that don't actively monitor political risk often perceive adverse events as "black swans," requiring much more dramatic or drastic shifts than they might have had to take if they had viewed changes as "gray rhinos"—that is, entirely in the realm of anticipated possibility. Fortunately, many executives are waking up to the new imperative: 44 percent of those focused on improving political risk management say that integrating political risk into ERM is the most important action their company could take.[96]

POLITICAL RISK IS HARD TO INTEGRATE—BUT IT CAN BE DONE

Many companies are already adept at recognizing, assessing, and managing various types of risk. But, to date, too few have managed to weave scan and focus for *political* risk into their more established efforts to manage the risk landscape they face. The failure to prioritize political risk is most evident at companies where efforts to manage political risk are largely superficial—an exercise designed to check a box, rather than to weave real oversight into a company's broader risk management process. We have seen many examples of this treatment, including at companies with otherwise sophisticated risk management processes, and we've noted several common pitfalls that trip up companies working to include political risk in broader risk management frameworks.

First, we often hear that risk teams are generally aware of political risk but are not sure how to approach the area given its daunting complexity. Executives sometimes share that they don't believe their company is able to properly manage political risk—so why should they use limited time and resources trying? Even at some globally recognized companies, there can be a perception that political risk developments are too broad and involve too many parties to be effectively managed by the business. In other situations, companies may not even share an internal understanding of what political risk means, or they may not know how to access and measure relevant data for these risks. Typically, the right starting point for these conversations is around scan and focus—these fundamentals usually deserve initial attention before executives turn to integrating political risk into broader risk management.

Second, we have found that political risk is too often lumped with macro-level financial risks, macroeconomic risks, ESG risks, or some other set of external risks. But when political risk is paired with macroeconomic modeling, the noneconomic factors—how a change in government might impact the market landscape or how a new trade agreement might shift global alliances, as examples—tend to get short shrift, especially if the risk management team does not quantify them in some way. And when managers lump external risk categories together in a single taxonomy, executives cannot distinguish one bucket from another. In one case, a consumer technology manufacturer defined its risk area as "geopolitical and macro socioeconomic factors and volatility," which included everything from regional wars to changes in consumer spending habits. By conflating these various risk areas, the risk category can become too broad, creating challenges for identifying triggers, assessing exposure, and recommending a substantive plan of action.

Even if political risk is a stand-alone entry in a risk management system, sometimes the way such systems capture political risks is too high level to be useful. Lumping all political risks into a single entry obscures the reality that different political risks pose different management challenges. The specificity of how political risks are identified and articulated is important. For instance, an election that brings into office a government with an entirely new domestic policy agenda will impact a company differently than if two countries impose new trade and investment restrictions—so these would require different risk management actions. In addition, separating out political risks allows risk managers to assess *combined* impacts. For instance, a change in government might auger big shifts in the availability of certain raw materials *and* in a country's commitment to maintaining a certain trade relationship *and* in destabilizing a nearby country that serves as an important market.

Finally, even when political risk is incorporated in a more meaningful way into a company's risk management process, it's often done in ways that leave value off the table. Rather than being the subject of perpetual scrutiny and updating—as might happen if commodity prices were particularly volatile or if a company's supply chain was being disrupted—companies often only revisit political risks as part of an annual risk assessment or when a question comes in from the board or another senior executive forum. As the evolution of globalization speeds up, management will have to adapt with more agility.

THREADING THE NEEDLE—HOW IT CAN BE DONE

Some companies *have* managed to weave political risk into their risk management programs in a more robust way. In one case, a company focused on Latin American markets differentiated "regulatory" and "political and economic uncertainty" as two separate risk areas, with different risk owners and processes mapped accordingly. While the latter still brought together the political and economic realms, the risk area was narrowly defined to focus on the impact to revenue and profitability—thus enabling effective risk management.

Sometimes, companies also seek to capture their management of certain political risks in a *public* way, by using annual reports and risk disclosures as strategic documents that address the macroenvironment in which they operate.[97] As just one example, Petrobras—a Brazil-based, state-owned petroleum company—explicitly states, in the risk factor section of its annual report on Form 10-K, that the Brazilian government's 64 percent stake of common stock has created political risk for the company itself. When the government changes hands, new members of the executive board and the board of directors are empowered to steer changes to both structure and strategy. But the company has also identified other political risks across the globe and their impacts on Petrobras. For instance, the 10-K points to the conflict between Ukraine and Russia as a key geopolitical risk that is likely to continue to impact fossil fuel prices, supply chains, and the global economy, which, as the company states, "could have an adverse effect on demand for our goods and services and the price of our securities."[98] This illustrates

Petrobras's commitment to considering political risk in both its home country and globally, especially regarding how the company is connected to its country's government.

TOOLS OF POLITICAL RISK MANAGEMENT

As revealed by the survey data discussed earlier, many executives and risk managers understand that geopolitical risk is growing. But as much as they don't want to miss an emerging risk, many worry that their company will lend too much credence to developments that aren't real threats. The challenge, then, is to sort the wheat from the chaff—not only to scan for all the political shifts or to determine, through focus, which political shifts could impact a specific part of a business, but to understand how to *manage* political risks. Fortunately, the last several years have illuminated internal strategies that can point executives and managers in the right direction. We explore five of them here, highlighting how they can be adapted to political risk management.

Dynamic political risk assessment

Executives can use a dynamic political risk assessment to distinguish which circumstances present more and less risk.[99] The first step is defining political risk and then analyzing a firm's inherent political risk and the management response gap. That requires inputs from multiple sources on a continual basis. This differs in two important ways from more traditional risk assessments, in which companies typically conduct interviews to identify risks and then create metrics in the form of key risk indicators (KRIs) on an annual basis. A dynamic political risk assessment, in contrast, leverages a wider array of internal and external data to identify a broader set of rapidly changing and emerging risks—and then continuously updates those assessments.

Data and information sources can include qualitative analyses and quantitative metrics. Internal sources can include stakeholder interviews, a review of the company's historical risk performance, and risk assessments performed within a particular business unit or region. External sources, such as news media monitoring and social media sentiment listening, can help to challenge any biases in the internal sources. Having compiled these elements, risk managers perform a comparative evaluation, with the resulting inventory evaluated against the axes in the following matrix (see figure 7).

FIGURE 7.
WHEN AND HOW TO RESPOND TO POLITICAL RISKS — AND WHEN TO ACCEPT THEM

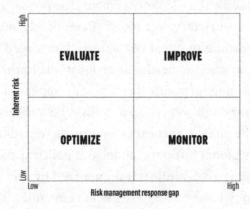

Source: "Risk management: When to respond and when to accept risk,"
EY website, https://www.ey.com/en_us/risk/when-to-respond-and-when-to-accept-risk.

With the various political risks placed in the appropriate quadrant, risk managers can begin to sort out how to approach different political risks. Those items placed in the "evaluate" quadrant should be reviewed against existing action plans. Those in the "improve" quadrant should be the focus of executive management and board reporting. Those in the "optimize" quadrant are viewed as being "overmanaged," meaning that risk managers should evaluate and reallocate resources if necessary. And, intuitively, those in the "monitor" quadrant require ongoing monitoring. Companies may choose to repeat these steps on a monthly, quarterly, or biannual basis. The frequency should reflect the organization's vulnerability to shifts and should be intentionally set by management.

Amid increasing awareness of the strategic necessity of political risk management, we find that companies are diverse in terms of where political risks broadly sit on such a matrix. We analyzed 350 public companies on their political risk exposure (inherent risk) and their level of political risk management (response gap) by using two proprietary data sets.[100] Remarkably, no strong trends regarding political risk approach emerged by sector, revenue size, or headquarter location. Rather, each company's specific political risk profile appeared to be a feature—although, crucially, not always a *deliberate* feature—of the choices that executives made regarding their company's global business model and political risk management activities. While not regularized by sector, size, or location, we were able to segment companies into four different profiles (see figure 8).

FIGURE 8.
FOUR TYPES OF COMPANIES EMERGE BASED ON
THEIR RELATIVE POLITICAL RISK EXPOSURE AND MANAGEMENT

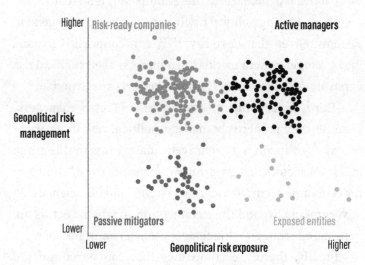

Note: Analysis of 356 companies. The majority (85%) reported revenue of US$1 billion or more. Each metric is on a scale from 0 (lowest) to 100 (highest). Across all companies on this matrix, political risk exposure ranged from 26 to 67; political risk management ranged from 28 to 88. For visualization purposes, the minimum and maximum values for each axis are set to illustrate variation between companies.

Source: "Why a level head is needed to deal with geopolitical risk," EY website, https://www.ey.com/en_gl/geostrategy/why-a-level-head-is-needed-to-deal-with-geopolitical-risk.

First, some companies are "passive mitigators," including companies that tend to be more globalized, and where diversification effectively mitigates political risks (assuming risks are uncorrelated along companies' supply chains or across key markets). Unfortunately, amid heightened volatility and uncertainty, passive mitigators are poorly positioned to respond to geopolitical shifts because they lack a strategic approach to political risk management. They are the least proactive group overall when it comes to scanning, focusing, and strategizing around political risk.

Second, some companies are "risk-ready." They have relatively low political risk exposure, but nevertheless are the most active risk managers. These companies tend to do a better job integrating political risk into broader risk management systems. Given that dexterity, they can confidently expand into strategic growth markets that increase their political risk exposure—if other factors in those markets are favorable.

Third, some companies were termed "active managers" because they proactively manage political risk in a variety of ways. Although not exclusively, many firms in this group hail from sectors that governments consider to be "strategic" for economic security, including energy and life sciences. As governments expand their conception of which sectors are considered strategic, this category may grow in number.

Finally, there are companies that can be considered "exposed entities" because they face the most problematic mismatch: high levels of political risk exposure and low-quality political risk management—a circumstance that is likely to lead to significant downside impacts on growth and limited new opportunities.

There are some advantages and disadvantages to each of these profiles. But no matter the circumstance, executives need to understand how to align their political risk capabilities with exposure levels. And amid an uncertain outlook for globalization, aligning political risk management capabilities with exposure levels is an increasing imperative. Engaging in a dynamic risk assessment is a useful tool in this process.

Quantification and dashboards

Companies looking to improve their risk management often find that they need to enhance their ability to track the probability that a risk will materialize, and the degree to which that materialized risk will have a material impact on the company. To do that effectively, risk management teams can identify KRIs and keep track of them in a dashboard. Good indicators change in an observable way and are connected to the causes of the risk analyzed in the risk assessment. The bulk of these indicators need to be quantitative so that they can be woven seamlessly into a company's other risk management activities.

Several challenges exist in identifying and tracking political risk KRIs as part of companies' horizon scanning systems. First, many publicly available indicators are produced only once a year, or even less frequently. (Although, as discussed in the Scan chapter, some private data providers are making notable advances in the quantification of more specific and frequent political risk indicators.) Second, indicators are sometimes not available for all countries of interest or are available only from certain circumscribed time periods. Third, they can be skewed by any biases within the organizations that produce them. For all these reasons, companies may find that the tracking of metrics for geostrategy is more challenging than in other more well-established risk areas. That said, efforts in this area can make including political risk in broader risk management systems easier.

Political risk indicators and dashboards can help a company's executives feel more confident that their political risk identification systems are fit for purpose. Executives should not rely solely on dashboards, however, as they can some-times oversimplify the risk environment. They are *most* use-ful when employed by companies that already have a range of political risk management tools in use, but whose risk manag-ers are unclear on how to extrapolate specific impacts. That's where outside help can be useful. When working with clients, EY teams often draw on a library of more than 150 publicly available political risk indicators to produce a custom basket tied to their sector, geographic footprint, and risk profile. We then work collaboratively to weave those political risk indica-tors into existing risk registries and connected risk systems. Dashboards can also be helpful in sparking deeper discus-sions between risk teams and the broader C-suite.

As one example, EY teams recently helped a company to create a geopolitical risk pillar within its ERM program. The company's board had identified geopolitical risk as an area that deserved heightened attention. To satisfy that demand, the company formalized its identification and evaluation processes, and assigned a risk owner to this area. EY teams then helped the company identify and develop four politi-cal risk scenarios. Using the political risk indicator database, analysts identified external KRIs and risk drivers for each, including the number of new discriminatory trade policies in the company's sector. The EY teams also helped the com-pany to identify internal KRIs to monitor, such as the annual volatility of an applied tariff rate and the number of annual supply disruptions. The C-suite was able to report to the board that it had defined both internal company metrics and external key risk metrics to track.

Loss modeling and stress testing

A loss modeling approach focuses on understanding the potential financial implication of a particular risk scenario bearing out. Applied to geopolitics, this could include assessing how future hypothetical developments may lead to financial costs for the company—in the form of investment or asset losses. This is often done through stress testing, which assesses an organization's resilience to unfavorable, but conceivable, circumstances. Applying stress tests is most typically used in financial services institutions, but it can be usefully applied to companies operating in other sectors as well. As organizations consider potential losses in particular geopolitical scenarios, leveraging the formalized structure and process of stress testing may be worthwhile. Of course, the ability to build scenarios containing realistic business consequences of potential political risk events in a quantifiable manner relies on a strong focus function.

One example of a geopolitical stress test could involve envisioning a potential conflict between two countries and how that could impact the business. Key assumptions for the scenario could include impacts to the economy of the company's home country, such as GDP loss, equity market declines, inflation impact, and fluctuation in the exchange rate. Further assumptions could include the length of the conflict and the period of time that a key product may experience export disruption. With the key assumptions assigned to the scenario set, geostrategists can then assess the business losses related to the scenario. Property damage losses in the affected conflict regions would be assigned a value. Investment portfolio impacts would be modeled out. And any potential talent disruptions would similarly be captured. These are but a few of the loss exposure types that a stress test would help to model out.

Importantly, stress testing should include consideration of the right time horizon for the scenario—or perhaps the comparison of multiple time horizons. A three-month test may raise very different business considerations and loss capture than a one-year scenario. This is because business elements, such as inventory shelf life and reputational impacts, would play out differently across various time horizons. For example, during the first few weeks of the conflict, prior stockpiling could protect against sales losses, but such losses are likely to be higher when stress testing a yearlong conflict. In this way, stress testing allows for calculating loss levels as well as providing key business insights that could be used to help defend the business against downside risk.

Loss modeling strategies also allow companies to hedge exposure through financial instruments and to more easily integrate political risk management into broader risk dashboards. One especially popular tool is political risk insurance, which is most useful for large capital expenditures in markets with higher levels of political risk. The loss modeling and stress testing approaches can help inform the level of political risk insurance a company may wish to purchase.

Scenario analysis

If a company is cognizant that political risks are likely to evolve over a certain period of time—say, five years—but is less certain of *how* those risks will evolve, managers can use scenario analysis to map out the possibilities. This is a strategic foresight methodology that enables the systematic assessment of future uncertainty through the exploration of multiple alternative futures. It involves developing engaging narratives of possible futures based on key uncertainties that a company has about its future operating environment. In this manner, it bolsters enterprise resilience. Most importantly, scenario analysis enables executives to identify immediate actions that can be taken to mitigate or manage future risks in the potential scenarios.

Scenario analysis is a multistep process and—like geostrategy overall—works best when it is a cross-functional exercise. The first step is to identify the elements driving heightened threats or opportunities through a horizon scanning exercise, which may be assisted by AI. That process also includes conducting preliminary research into an organization's strategic questions and noting key uncertainties over a specified timeframe. Next, risk managers should sketch out scenarios by conducting additional research and conjecturing how relevant outcomes might be affected by interactions between the various drivers. Finally, those insights should be integrated into risk management, with the broader implications of any proposed mitigation considered against a wider array of challenges.

Scenario analysis is most useful when a company faces a complex, uncertain future and leaders want to challenge current assumptions about the risks they face. EY teams helped one client use this tool by designing a set of scenarios that might impact an important market. Regional and sector analysts helped to identify drivers and signposts—namely what real-world events might favor one scenario over another. The team then analyzed the impact of each of the scenarios on the client's supply chain, revenues, human resources, and government relations. This gave the company's executives a clearer picture of the extent of the risk and its quantitative value. Finally, the team created a set of recommendations for how the company could act today to mitigate the potential downside impacts of such scenarios and more proactively manage the political risks they faced. This scenario analysis also positioned the company's executive team to create a risk management playbook that could be utilized if a downside scenario materialized in the future.

Tabletop simulations

Finally, those looking to improve a company's risk management can employ either tabletop simulation or war-gaming—techniques in which individuals within a company play through their responses to potential scenarios. In tabletop exercises, stakeholders from different functions or teams within an organization gather to discuss a potential political risk event, with the goals being information sharing and collaborative risk response formulation. War-gaming provides a more intense experience, enabling participants to act out how they would respond in a simulated political risk crisis scenario. The latter often employs previously unannounced "injects" to stress the company's response plans and processes.

These techniques are most helpful when risk managers have clarity on a type of risk that might emerge in the future, but are less clear on the specifics, how the company would be affected through primary, secondary, and tertiary effects, and, ultimately, how the company would respond. These methodologies are also helpful in siloed organizations, where various teams have taken ownership over a portion of risk that could affect those in other silos. Those caught within these silos will undoubtedly come into contact if, in fact, certain political risk events come to pass. Simulations and war games allow them to get to know each other, building camaraderie and ways of working together to prepare *before* a crisis hits.

Using these tools, EY teams helped a company with significant exposure in China play out how a deterioration in US-China relations could affect the business. The EY teams presented the client with a series of hypothetical scenarios. Based on feedback, the team then worked with the client to design a single hypothetical scenario with multiple levels of severity. The ERM team convened a workshop attended by the full risk committee as well as cross-functional and cross-regional business representation. The event prompted an effort to build a future risk response "playbook" that could be woven into the company's ERM and presented to the board.

WHAT GOOD POLITICAL RISK MANAGEMENT LOOKS LIKE

Given changing geopolitical circumstances, there's little doubt that political risk will grow for most corporations as a strategic priority. With these tools at their disposal, C-suites and boards need to ask themselves what value they most want to glean from the risk management process. How can inherent political risks best be tracked and residual risk levels best be managed on an ongoing basis? We've found that the most effective way to account for political risk weaves any new analysis into existing connected risk approaches and internal audit processes, using both qualitative and quantitative indicators to monitor identified risks and help spot emerging issues.

For many companies, political risk management is ripe to become a source of competitive advantage. The EY *Geostrategy in Practice 2021* survey found less than one-quarter of global executives believed their company integrates political risk management into broader risk management on a regular or proactive basis.[101] But in the EY *CEO Imperative Study 2021*, more than 40 percent of executives revealed they intend to adjust their risk management practices—the top area of change overall. CEOs prioritized data-driven analytics (61 percent) and focusing on existential strategic risks (49 percent) within the context of planned changes to risk management.[102] By working with risk teams, C-suites can better manage these strategic risks—including, of course, political risk—both by protecting the business from threats and by identifying new opportunities over the horizon.

In time, companies that do political risk management well will develop systems that make the process feel almost like second nature. The tools above won't be one-offs, but will be perpetually iterative. The key, in the end, is integration. By leveraging the political risk identification outputs from the scan process and the tangible estimations of political risk impact developed through focus, this enables managers to prioritize which risks (on both the downside and the upside) demand the most attention—namely those in the upper right corner of a probability vs. impact matrix (see figure 9). Then managers will be equipped to target the right set of strategies to manage the political risks the company faces. Of course, such a picture captures risk likelihood and impact at a specific moment in time. Such assessments need to be updated dynamically in real time, particularly as the velocity of how each risk evolves will differ in important ways.

FIGURE 9.
ILLUSTRATIVE POLITICAL RISK MANAGEMENT MATRIX BASED ON SCAN (LIKELIHOOD) AND FOCUS (IMPACT) ANALYSES

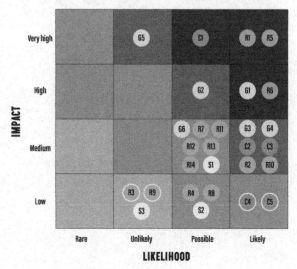

Source: EY Geostrategic Business Group.

This integrated approach enables elements of political risk to be addressed collectively, helping to minimize the impact of downside events while also proactively identifying upside opportunities. And that points to the final way that political risk management can be used—by incorporating the results into company strategy, the subject we'll turn to next. As the C-suite and the board become more cognizant of political risks, they can use that intelligence to create strategies to capture long-term competitive advantage for their business.

4

STRATEGIZE

Incorporate political risk
analysis into strategic decisions

In 2013, a variety of political risk and market developments prompted the global fashion industry to re-evaluate its supply chain strategies and explore alternative sourcing locations (not unlike manufacturers seeking to diversify global supply chains today). Many global clothing producers began looking for manufacturing partners in new markets—places where the labor would be affordable and where executives could have confidence in managing a variety of risks. An alternative emerged as a particularly attractive one: Ethiopia.

Ethiopia's appeal was clear. Wages were much lower than the market rate for workers in many parts of Asia due to differences in living costs. And the Horn of Africa, in particular, had the resource endowments not only to manufacture the clothing, but also to grow the cotton that would be used as raw material—a commodity often imported to traditional sourcing markets in Asia.[103] Geographic proximity to certain sales markets, such as Europe, provided further appeal. In short, from the perspective of a traditional market assessment,

Ethiopia appeared like a hidden gem—a place where labor was affordable and resources were plentiful.

Moreover, the Ethiopian government appeared eager to incentivize foreign investment—and to construct the dams, railways, and roads necessary to make global commerce possible.[104] And so, by 2014, a whole range of large global clothing manufacturers and brands were investing in Ethiopian facilities.[105] The investments were, in many cases, substantial: companies built large facilities with the expectation that those plants would produce clothing years into the future, with out-year savings driving a long-term profit.

But by late 2020, only a few years after foreign companies had begun investing in Ethiopian facilities, the business environment in Ethiopia began to shift. It wasn't that the global market for fashion had changed or that the cost of labor in Ethiopia was rising faster than economists had expected—those sorts of risks had been properly accounted for through the traditional due diligence done prior to investments. Rather, what emerged was an explicit *political* risk: civil war broke out, even drawing in the military of the neighboring country Eritrea.[106] The effects were immediate and devastating for those living in and near Ethiopia. And the conflict had very significant implications for the clothing companies operating there.

Several facilities in and around Tigray, the northern region most directly engulfed in the violence, were put in immediate peril. Many foreign companies suspended operations and flew their foreign staff out of Ethiopia. Since most of the fighting was restricted to the Tigray region, some companies with locations in the other parts of the country could continue operating. But the civil conflict risked affecting those companies' operations and reputations as well. Less than a decade after the Ethiopia experiment had begun en masse for the fashion industry, its success was put in jeopardy by rising political risks.

Of course, it is easy to have 20/20 vision in hindsight. By many measures, the Ethiopia investment had been strategically sound. The labor market had been competitive. The government subsidies had appeared attractive. The supply chain links were strong. The underlying infrastructure was improving. Ethiopia appeared a good candidate for supply chain diversification. But it seems that *political risk* may have been a blind spot for some companies. And that, in the end, had left them vulnerable to unforeseen strategic risks.[107]

No strategic move is without risk. Companies rarely make investments, expand their footprints, merge with other corporations, or diversify their supply chains without taking on some chance of things shifting down the line. And many companies have developed sophisticated models to help them navigate what are often complex circumstances. But now the prevalence of political risk and the materiality of its impacts on business outcomes are becoming more significant. We argue that political volatility has elevated the importance of geopolitics to corporate strategies to its highest level in a generation. And it's for that reason that companies can benefit from incorporating political risks more centrally into the creation and execution of their strategies.

WHY INCORPORATE POLITICAL RISK INTO STRATEGY

Successfully weaving political dynamics into corporate strategy is becoming a powerful source of competitive advantage. Already, the depth and breadth of global change—and the impacts on strategy—have begun to crystalize. The COVID-19 pandemic drove many governments to tighten foreign direct investment (FDI) regulations, impose export restrictions on critical products, and incentivize the reshoring or nearshoring of strategic supply chains in the pursuit of "self-reliance" and resiliency. Executives told us in 2021 that their companies were making a variety of corporate strategy shifts in response to the pandemic (see figure 10).[108] The greatest number of firms responded by diversifying their supplier bases. In other cases, companies have responded by retrenching to domestic markets. And that hasn't meant less M&A activity so much as it has meant a different flavor of corporate activity; nearly twice as many companies planned to increase domestic M&A as did those that planned to decrease it following the pandemic.[109]

These strategic decisions, of course, were snapshots in time—reactions in the corporate world to immediate upheavals born from a global pandemic. But they reflect a larger trend. EY surveys global CEOs every year, and the changing results in recent years speak to fundamental strategic changes. In February 2021, 82 percent of global CEOs responded "yes" to the following question: Are you altering your strategic investments as a result of geopolitical challenges? About two years later, that figure had risen to 97 percent.[110] And by mid-2023, 99 percent of CEOs were

FIGURE 10.
PANDEMIC-RELATED POLITICAL RISKS BEGAN
TO DRIVE CORPORATE STRATEGY SHIFTS

How do you anticipate trade protectionism and industrial policies in response to the COVID-19 pandemic will affect your company's supply chain, M&A, and market entry strategy in the next 12 months?

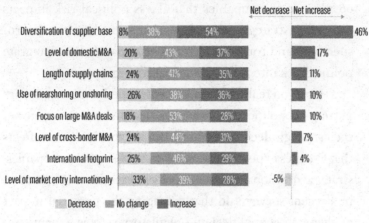

Source: EY Geostrategy in Practice 2021.

reporting that their companies planned to alter different aspects of their strategies as a result of geopolitical challenges—40 percent were delaying a planned investment, 40 percent were reconfiguring supply chains, and 34 percent were exiting businesses in certain markets altogether.[111]

This demonstrates that companies are incorporating geopolitical risks into current strategy. Indeed, as early as 2021, companies were doing more to incorporate political risk into strategy than any other aspect of the geostrategy framework. Political risk was proactively included in strategic decisions—including market entry and transactions—by about half of the companies surveyed, and only 2 percent of executives said that their companies do not incorporate political risk analysis into market entry and exit or transactions decisions.[112] But if C-suites have begun to realize that their strategies need political risk inputs, many still have a great deal of work to do before they are at the vanguard. That's largely because a gap remains between the 66 percent of companies that assess political risk impacts on *current* strategy—something that is, by definition, retrospective—and roughly half of the companies that integrate political risk into *forward-looking* strategic planning.

Here, you really have to look into whether companies are putting geopolitics and other political risks at the center of their strategic decision-making. Despite the significant effects that C-suites expect political risk to have on their companies' strategic decisions, only a minority of executives (14 percent) in a recent survey said that managing the potential impact of changing geopolitical and regulatory risks is a main strategic consideration today.[113] So, while the impact of political dynamics on strategic decisions is widely understood, executives are much less likely to consider this level of analysis as critical to precisely those processes. Boards similarly tend to pay more regular attention to the impact of political risk on *existing* strategy (40 percent) than on incorporating political risk into *new* business decisions (25 percent). In other words, companies too often simply talk about political risk when forming strategy without paying it sufficient heed.

At a macro level, that roughly half of companies are failing to weave political risk into long-term strategic planning is undoubtedly a cause for concern. But for individual firms, it represents a strategic opportunity. If an investor or business can properly manage political risk in a market where competitors cannot, or will not, then there is a potential path toward gaining competitive advantage. In other words, some companies may view markets prone to political risk as high-risk, high-reward situations. There is some question as to whether C-suites would treat such acumen as a durable source of competitive advantage, particularly in the face of a significant political risk event. But the 45 percent of companies that plan to invest in identifying, evaluating, and responding to emerging risks have a clear opportunity to outperform their competition.[114]

Changing geopolitical dynamics

Today, the re-emergence of significant geopolitical risk makes any company that is overly dependent on a single supplier or the success of an investment panning out in a single market vulnerable. The corporate world's decades-long focus on building just-in-time dynamics will increasingly shift to the imperatives of "just in case." Put another way: strategists, who once prioritized *efficiency*, are now balancing that imperative with a new commitment to *resilience*. They can't assume that maximizing profit now will maximize profit later because the geopolitical circumstances later may turn things upside down. Executives need to anticipate geopolitical shifts and design strategies to compete in the future—just as Toyota did in the last wave of global upheaval, as discussed in the introduction.

These changes today have the potential to affect many aspects of corporate strategy. The global marketplace is increasingly characterized by nationalized "industrial policies" designed to enhance a country's ability to produce and maintain certain critical technologies and other products viewed as strategic to national and economic security. Governments are increasingly offering preferential financing, reduced tax rates, or other incentives to onshore production. These supply chain shifts—referred to as nearshoring, onshoring, and friendshoring—are incentivizing many companies to reassess their home-country government's network of alliances and trade agreement partners simply because companies are likely to face lower levels of geopolitical risk in "friendly" markets.

An additional challenge

That points to the additional challenge of incorporating political risk into strategy today. Media headlines and political risk commentators tend to focus on *geopolitical* risks because they embody the systemic change that's occurring in the international system. But, as we discussed in the Scan chapter, geopolitics is only one level of political risk. There are three other types of political risks that strategists *also* need to take into account: country, regulatory, and societal. The Ethiopia story illustrates this. And, in part due to geopolitical dynamics, these risks are in flux as well.

Take, as an example, the war in Ukraine. In the immediate aftermath of Russia's invasion in 2022, many corporate executives began looking to invest in other nearby Central European and Eastern European countries. The challenge of exiting Russia and finding alternatives for Ukraine-based production, much of which had gone offline, was urgent and multifaceted. Given the urgency of the situation, there was appeal in assuming the alternative markets in the region were monolithic. But of course, the countries near and around Ukraine each had important economic and political dynamics of their own. So, companies needed, in short order, to get a grasp of not only supplier ecosystems, talent pools, and costs, but also tax and industrial policies, election outlooks, sociopolitical dynamics, regulatory risks, and more. And then it was necessary to compare all of these dynamics to the possibility of pursuing markets in geographies farther away. In short, it wasn't only geopolitical risks that mattered to strategic production location and market entry decisions—but the full suite of political risks that companies could face in any new market.

And, for that reason, executives need a better and more holistic understanding of which countries' political and policy environments provide the best long-term growth opportunities. They need a deeper feel for where they can create the most sustainable long-term value. Strategists need to place increased emphasis on asking a new set of geostrategic questions, such as these: Where does my home-country government's policies allow or incentivize production? Which governments support growth in my sector, and are there any reputational risks associated with selling there? In short, as the global landscape has become more complex, resilient strategies have become more complicated to design because there are more political risk factors to consider.

The basics of strategy

To understand *how* to weave political risk into strategy, you need first to *define* strategy. Henry Mintzberg defines it as "a pattern in a stream of decisions."[115] Michael Porter argues: "Strategy is the creation of a unique and valuable position, involving a different set of activities," contending that its "essence . . . is choosing to perform activities differently than rivals do."[116] And Felix Oberholzer-Gee defines it as "a plan to create value."[117]

Although there is wisdom in all these answers, from a political risk perspective, it is helpful to see strategy defined by two key questions. First, which markets should the company operate in or sell to? The "market" encompasses all the geographic territories where a company's many tentacles extend—those in which suppliers are located, products are produced, sales are carried out, or other corporate assets are housed. It also comprises all the elements across which the company competes: products, services, channels, customers, and so on.

Second, strategy is defined by how a company intends to compete and win in those markets. How will it position itself in terms of drawing competitive advantages from great procurement or efficient logistics or innovative product design or something else—and how will the company maintain those advantages? This second part centers, in essence, on the "how" of a company's operations. These choices should all fit together in a way that makes a clear, cohesive whole. To that end, as our EY-Parthenon colleagues argue, strategy should be simple enough to fit on a page (see figure 11).

FIGURE 11.
A SIMPLE "STRATEGY ON A PAGE" ENABLES A COMPANY TO FOCUS ON
WHAT TO DO — AND, JUST AS IMPORTANTLY, WHAT *NOT* TO DO

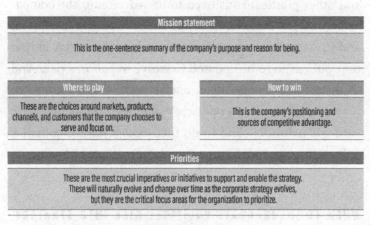

Source: EY-Parthenon.

While there are many overlapping elements between manage and strategize activities, executives tasked with overseeing risk management are generally focused on challenges that are *already* present—namely the elements where risk currently exists for the business. Executives focused on strategy, by contrast, aim to look beyond the current business landscape and seize *future* opportunities. Although both are a mix of offense and defense, strategy is more tilted toward offense—seizing the opportunities associated with an uncertain future rather than protecting against an unforeseen change. There is an overlap between the tasks a company performs to manage and, alternatively, to strategize. But these activities, while both crucial, are nevertheless distinct.

Companies, of course, have long worked to improve their ability to plan and strategize with a focus on long-term success. So, the new focus on political risk should not be viewed as a *replacement* for the approaches that have long prevailed in strategic planning. Rather, geopolitical trends and other political risks need to be woven into the company's strategic decision-making. Indeed, risk management and strategy share an important commonality today in that they *both* need to be updated to weave in *political* risk. And so that's today's imperative: boards and executives need to execute plans to weave political risk more directly into their strategic planning. And to do that *thoughtfully*, companies will need to commit to pursuing that goal *systematically*.

WHEN TO INCORPORATE POLITICAL RISK INTO STRATEGY

When a company formulates its strategy—when it seeks to answer these two strategic questions—or when it makes a strategic decision about a specific investment, executives need to incorporate political risk from the very beginning. Every successful business strategy is underpinned by an in-depth understanding of both the industry dynamics and the competitive landscape in which a company sits—and *both* are increasingly being influenced by political risk. For that reason, before the C-suite makes decisions about which markets to be in and how to compete in those markets, executives need to incorporate the intelligence derived from scan and focus. If political risk needs to be included from the beginning of any strategic process, it also needs to be woven in throughout the process, in specific ways (see figure 12). To that end, executives need to understand the specific actions, tools, and methodologies at their disposal.

But before focusing on the means of incorporating political risk into strategy, let's first identify the various business decisions when consideration of political risk is warranted.

When pursuing transactions

Executives need to weave political risk into their deliberations when considering any significant transaction, particularly when a merger, acquisition, joint venture, or spin-off crosses borders. Leaders typically first consider whether a potential transaction fits within a company's overall strategy. In the case of a merger, acquisition, or partnership, those in a company's strategy team then identify the right target, minimize any associated risks, develop a plan to prevent value erosion, and accelerate potential synergies. In the case of a spin-off, strategists ask whether divestment puts the company in a

FIGURE 12.
STRATEGIZE: INCORPORATE POLITICAL
RISK ANALYSIS INTO OPERATIONS AND STRATEGY

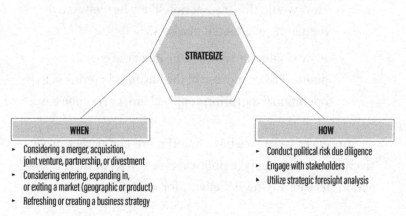

Source: EY Geostrategic Business Group.

better position and how executives can garner a price that positions the company well to raise capital for future investments. These are standard steps of due diligence.

But while these considerations remain necessary, they are not *sufficient*. Given the new presence of heightened political risk, executives need to place greater weight on the answers to a range of geostrategic questions about the transaction, such as the following:

- Is the target or acquiring company in a sector considered "strategic" by any government in the markets being evaluated?

- How could the geopolitical relations with the home country's government of the target or acquiring company affect stakeholder perceptions of the transaction?

- Does the target or acquiring company have any contracts or relations with any government entities?

- How would this transaction likely be viewed by regulators in affected markets?

- How would this transaction affect the overall political risk exposure of the business in terms of its operational footprint, supply chain, or revenue base?

In recent years, we have noted more companies proactively seeking to analyze political risk as part of their transaction decisions. One EY client, for example, was recently presented with an opportunity to acquire a company in Eastern Europe. Beyond carrying out ordinary due diligence, the company wanted to understand political risks, explicitly delineating the new exposures the combined company would have across different dimensions (geopolitical, country, regulatory, and societal). In essence, C-suite executives wanted to understand what key *political* considerations would impact both the proposed integration and any future business operations, and EY teams collaborated with the company's leaders to think through those challenges using some of the tools explored in more detail below. When the deal was ultimately announced, executives had a much better handle on what they faced ahead, including insights that empowered them to anticipate and prepare for a range of potential political risks associated with acquiring the other company.

When entering and exiting markets

To boost long-term growth prospects, executives often explore new markets—opportunities to expand into new geographies to set up operations, engage new suppliers, identify new channels, target new customer segments, or even create new product categories. The incorporation of political risk into such strategic decisions applies most significantly to entering or exiting a new geography—and, in certain cases, such as in sectors deemed strategic by governments, to entering a new product category. To evaluate each potential strategic move, companies must weigh the potential costs and benefits of entering a market, including any downstream impacts on existing customers, products, services, and processes. The same logic holds for when companies consider *exiting* a market.

Here, too, political risk is an increasingly influential consideration. Particularly when considering geographic expansion, executives must ask questions such as these:

- What political risks would my company be exposed to if it enters or expands in the market? Alternatively, how would exiting shift my company's levels of exposure across other markets?

- What policy incentives would my company be able to capitalize on if it entered or expanded in the market?

- Would exiting the market create any policy or regulatory compliance challenges?

- How would changing my company's presence in the market be viewed by the local stakeholders, including policymakers, regulators, customers, employees, and investors?

- How would the governments in other markets in which my company operates react to my company's shifting presence in the market?

- How would my customers, staff, and suppliers react to my company's shifting presence in the market?

Many have speculated about whether political risks are driving companies to enter or exit a particular market. But the analysis is also useful when taking a comparative view across several potential markets as a measure of differentiation. For instance, a company was considering whether to establish new operational locations. After narrowing down its options to two potential new manufacturing locations, the company's leadership paused to explore the political risk environment, the various socioeconomic trends in the two locations, and the probability of high-level impacts on operations of the identified risks in a comparative way. EY teams worked to assess the geopolitical, country, regulatory, and societal risks in both locations—at both the national and local levels—developing a bespoke political risk assessment to compare political risk probabilities and impacts if the manufacturer were to enter each market. Coupled with the other market entry analysis, this political risk exercise enabled the company's C-suite to make a better-informed strategic decision about which market to enter.

When refreshing or creating a business strategy

When companies are reviewing existing strategy and setting new strategic goals, they answer the two fundamental questions outlined above about where to compete and how to gain or maintain competitive advantage. In doing so, strategy teams typically analyze industry dynamics, such as market size, market growth, and the market share of leading competitors. The resulting intelligence can help executives identify the company's unique competitive advantages, while offering management clues on how to align all business units and functions to achieve strategic objectives. Designing strategy also increasingly includes articulating a company's purpose. In doing so, executives can galvanize and align employees, shareholders, communities, partners, and other stakeholders.

Again, while such strategic planning exercises are generally a great benefit, in the absence of a more serious consideration of political risks as part of the process, a great deal can be lost. For that reason, when thinking through strategy in a holistic way, company executives should also ask this series of politically oriented questions:

- Does the likely future political risk environment necessitate a re-evaluation of our mission statement and source of long-term value?

- Will political risk trends and events create new risks and opportunities that require a realignment of our global footprint or our corporate growth strategy?

- How will likely future political risks affect our operating model and supply chain strategy?

- How are political risk trends and events likely to impact my company's strategic advantages or disadvantages?

- Does my company have the resilience in its capital structure to succeed in the future political risk environment?

As an example, a company that produces an input used in the production of EV batteries recognized that its external environment was shifting. The emergence of the net-zero movement and geopolitical pressures were prompting turnover among the company's investors. Customers' and competitors' behaviors were creating structural changes in its markets. And the shift was particularly acute in the US, where raw material availability, domestic manufacturing capacity, and dependence on foreign supplies were all in flux. The company was aware that the political landscape was changing and wanted to redefine its notion of success by identifying new value opportunities through a clear, fact-based assessment of the global environment, customer demand, technology impacts, and, crucially, the risks born from government policy and politics.

Working with the company's strategy team, EY teams analyzed recent geopolitical, policy, and regulatory developments, with an emphasis on how the US Inflation Reduction Act of 2022 was likely to affect the company. The team also assessed likely future trends in the policy environment and other political risks affecting the company's sector in the US (e.g., societal risks). The analysis helped to inform a strategy designed to minimize downside risks and capture opportunities associated with these political changes.

HOW TO INCORPORATE POLITICAL RISK INTO STRATEGY

If it's now clear *why* we need to incorporate political risk into strategy, and *when* to work proactively to weave the intelligence born from scan and focus into forward-looking strategic decisions, we'll now turn to *how* best to carry it out. For most companies, strategy will be a broadly familiar concept. But because this function is applied in various companies in disparate ways, any individual company's plan of action, when threading political risk through existing strategic decision-making processes, will vary one to the next. Strategists can choose to embrace a variety of methodologies and approaches. Here, we highlight three common strategic decision-making tools or methodologies in which, in our experience, it is particularly useful to incorporate political risk assessments. Most importantly, though, the strategize aspect of geostrategy should be done in a proactive and iterative way—it is too important for the long-term strategic positioning of companies to be treated ad hoc.

Due diligence

First, companies should seek to weave political risk into their process when scrutinizing whether to shift markets (e.g., an entrance or exit) or pursue a transaction (such as an acquisition or a divestment). "Diligence," as this process is generally termed, includes several aspects: financial, tax, commercial, operational, IT, and cyber, among others. It is designed to help a strategy team identify value drivers associated with the transaction or market shift, improve deal structures, and mitigate risks. Today, that needs to include giving decision-makers a deeper and more expansive understanding of the role political risks will play in shaping the success of any strategic move (see figure 13).

Some companies already include a political risk module in their due diligence efforts around M&A and other transactions. Political risk intelligence can be similarly helpful in cases of conducting diligence for a potential market entry or exit. The first step in either case—as with geostrategy in general—is to scan for political risks associated with the target company or market. Those crafting corporate strategy need

FIGURE 13.
POLITICAL RISK DILIGENCE IS PART OF
AN INTEGRATED DUE DILIGENCE PROCESS

Integrated due diligence	
Commercial	**Financial**
▸ How can the transaction help address changing customer demands, or enhance the brand or market position? ▸ What incremental markets, customers, or sales channels will be created?	▸ What is the right data to support our forecast? ▸ How do differences in accounting policy affect the bottom-line profitability? ▸ Are there any balance sheet, off-balance-sheet, or accounting concerns?
Operational	**IT and cybersecurity**
▸ What are the sources and timing of synergies, and how are they quantified? ▸ How will we integrate operations, and how much will it cost?	▸ How can we assess existing IT capabilities for access to new markets and operational improvements? ▸ What are the cybersecurity and data privacy risks in our valuation?
Human resources	**Tax**
▸ How can roles and responsibilities be structured to maximize retention of key employees? ▸ Are there costs associated with redundancies? ▸ How will we design compensation and benefits programs that align with our vision and culture?	▸ Do we have a tax-efficient structure and a globally coordinated approach to deliver the commercial objectives and investment rationale?
Political risk	
▸ Scan: What geopolitical, country, regulatory, or societal risks could affect the viability or approval of the transaction? What political risks could affect the value of the investment in the medium to long term? ▸ Focus: How could these political risks impact the core business operations underpinning the transaction value? How could they affect the ability to achieve projected growth? ▸ Manage: Do we have the appropriate risk management structure and stakeholder awareness to manage new exposures?	

Source: EY Geostrategic Business Group; "Ask these M&A due diligence questions before signing a deal," EY website, https://www.ey.com/en_us/strategy-transactions/ask-these-m-a-due-diligence-questions-before-signing-a-deal.

to ask themselves this question: What policies or regulations could threaten compliance or erode transaction value? The key is to unearth the political risks that will be novel for the company if this move is executed. As discussed in the Scan chapter, this analysis will involve a wide array of sources and input from subject matter experts.

Once those risks have been identified, strategists need then to focus on how these political developments could affect a company if the transaction or market entry proceeds. This begins with assessing sector-wide impact. How would the political risks affect the market's economic outlook and the industry's growth prospects? Diligence then needs to focus on the company itself. How (if at all) does the political risk affect the company's ability to achieve projected growth? As discussed in the Focus chapter, this should include insights from operations, sales, and other functions.

Next, strategists must determine how risk management activities may need to evolve in the scenario in which the transaction or market shift is executed. How would the company manage the high-probability, high-impact political risks that have been identified? Would any of the new political risks the company could be exposed to balance or offset current risks? Strategists should collaborate with risk managers to combine all the scan and focus analysis, assess inherent and residual risks, and consider how to actively manage the most important risks going forward. Last, strategists should assess the underlying issue's impact on broader company strategy. Given a particular political risk assessment, how well does transaction or market entry fit with the company's overall strategy?

A company was recently considering whether to enter a new market via a joint venture (JV), through a wholly owned venture, or through some third alternative. By quantifying and evaluating the host government's political will to nurture its industry, which was seen as strategic by governments—and examining various ESG considerations of energy access, labor unionization issues, and several other potential challenges—the company's leaders gained the visibility needed to determine how their identified market opportunity aligned with political risk trends. EY teams helped the company's leadership by inventorying country-level political risks, subnational political risks in several different potential factory locations, and the geopolitical risks faced by the project.

Through this political risk due diligence process, the company's executives gleaned a sophisticated understanding of the political risks that could affect the value of the investment going forward, and how those political risks might affect not only investment strategy but also day-to-day operational strategy. By identifying, in greater detail, both potential pitfalls and unforeseen opportunities, the executives were prompted to think thoroughly about their risk appetite and their stakeholder management needs. This more holistic picture helped shape the C-suite's investment strategy and, ultimately, the JV partner negotiation.

Stakeholder engagement

As globalization continues to evolve, the political dimension of corporate strategy will increasingly become a lynchpin for executives eager to engage their stakeholders, including policymakers, regulators, civil society groups, employees, investors, and customers. By starting with corporate purpose, and successively taking inventory of their evolving responsibilities to various stakeholders, companies can address more explicitly how political risks will materially impact business functions. From there, they can plan and adjust strategy to incorporate these responsibilities and risks.[118]

When it comes to stakeholder engagement, the first step is to identify all the stakeholders—the people or groups who play a role in determining the outcome of the company's activities—a company has in any given market. Often, that means creating a stakeholder map delineating how salient the company's investment or activity is to each stakeholder, as well as how much power they have to influence the company's success (see figure 14). The resulting picture can help executives determine whether each stakeholder is likely to play a cooperative or oppositional role as the company pursues its agenda—and which stakeholder relationships require the most active engagement.

Once strategists understand their stakeholders' issues, they can flip the unit of analysis from the individual stakeholders to the issues they raised. Looking across the various issues of concern, they can ask these questions:

- Which issues overlap or share commonalities? Which show up in clusters?

- Do the various stakeholders align or conflict on issues?

- Beyond any holistic pattern, how do the stakeholders and their issues affect the company's strategy via a specific project or investment?

- How can the company prioritize stakeholders' expectations?

Companies should determine which stakeholders' expectations can be met with existing business strategy and

FIGURE 14.
A STAKEHOLDER PRIORITIZATION MATRIX HELPS
EXECUTIVES TARGET KEY RELATIONSHIPS

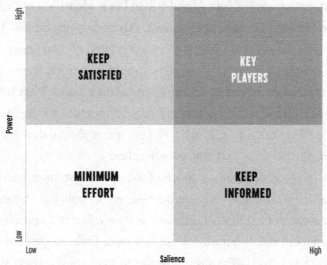

Source: Henisz, Witold J., *Corporate Diplomacy: Building Reputations and Relationships with External Stakeholders* (Sheffield: Greenleaf Publishing Limited, 2014).

143

FIGURE 15.
A STAKEHOLDER ISSUE MAP CAN HELP
EXECUTIVES PRIORITIZE POLITICAL ISSUES

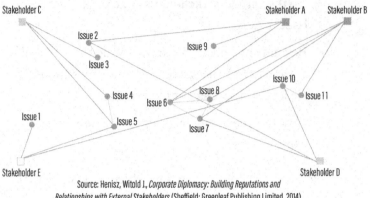

Source: Henisz, Witold J., *Corporate Diplomacy: Building Reputations and Relationships with External Stakeholders* (Sheffield: Greenleaf Publishing Limited, 2014).

operations, and which may require adjustments. Strategists should then assess which adjustments to the investment or project are most critical (see figure 15). In figure 15, for instance, stakeholders A and B had been identified as "key players" in the stakeholder map. Issues are placed on the map based on how closely they are related to one another. So, in this example, strategists should prioritize issues in two clusters: issues 6, 7, and 8, and issues 2 and 3 because these closely related issues are most important to the "key player" stakeholders. Finally, the company should develop a communications and engagement plan.

In many companies, much of the above is standard practice in stakeholder engagement—even if political dimensions are not explicitly taken into account. But it's a problem if political risk is left out of the equation. Only 55 percent of executives in a 2021 survey reported that they proactively develop trusted stakeholder relationships to manage political risks, and only 26 percent of them do so at the functional or business unit level.[119] That suggests that companies are not exerting enough effort to identify the political actors with an interest in the company's actions at the national, subnational, or local levels, including elected officials, regulators, and civil society leaders. And that can lead to blind spots.

Importantly, when engaging with stakeholders, executives need to be careful to build inclusive, participatory, and broad-based stakeholder coalitions rather than relying on an overly narrow set of stakeholders that could be seen as "insiders." Although the latter approach may facilitate a quicker market entry, this more limited stakeholder engagement can feed into historical grievances by those left out of the process and can elicit a political backlash. A stronger and broader coalition enables companies to survive elections, regime changes, and even populist pressures. The long-term value built through stakeholder relationships is key to sustaining growth, with stakeholder concerns informing broader strategic decision-making.

One public example of strategists implementing broad-based stakeholder engagement is Anglo American, a multinational mining company, which has long leveraged political risk assessments to create what it labels its Socio-Economic Assessment Toolbox (SEAT), designed to help the company assess its political environment in a geography.[120] When engaging in this process, Anglo American spends up to two years unpacking the political environment, employing anthropologists and others to map out issues and relationships. And while that endeavor doesn't directly eliminate the political challenges of embracing any given strategy, it reduces the level of residual risk that Anglo American faces ahead of each major investment step and enables the company to make strategy adjustments at the outset—before major risks are manifested.[121] That's because this process improves the overall impact of a project on the local community—a worthwhile strategic goal in its own right.

Another type of stakeholder engagement is exemplified by a company that worked with EY teams to assess the prevailing policies and regulations in four key markets. At the time, the company was exposed, on several fronts, to changes in its sector, which was undergoing a period of intense change around the world. Executives therefore realized that they needed to enhance the political sensitivities of their stakeholder engagement efforts with policymakers and regulators. Three potential approaches on a spectrum of involvement levels were identified in consultation with EY teams.

First, the company could engage simply as a *rule taker*, monitoring regulators' actions without trying to modify them in a proactive way. This option carried the lowest operational cost, but was weighed down by the disadvantage that access to real-time information and influence would be limited. It also meant de facto acceptance of the regulatory risks inherent to the markets of operation.

Second, the company could opt to be an *indirect rule shaper*, participating in relevant industry associations and organizations that were directly involved in policymaker and regulator engagement. This option provided an opportunity for the company to gather intelligence from the outside-in, but ongoing monitoring would require personnel and resources for coordination. Moreover, rule shaping would demand both global and local government relations capabilities, but would also offer the potential for collaboration within the industry ecosystem.

Finally, the company could opt to be a *direct rule shaper*, involving itself in direct advocacy with relevant regulators and other government stakeholders. This last option provided the potential for greater influence, but was sure to come at a higher cost, require greater coordination across government relations professionals, demand oversight and integration with strategy and operations, and call for more board and C-suite sponsorship and leadership.

After internal deliberations, company executives chose to pursue an *indirect rule shaper* role because it fit best with the company's overall strategy. This particular approach to stakeholder engagement with policymakers and regulators ensured the company's views would be "in the room" for major decisions, without raising the company's public profile beyond what C-suite executives thought was prudent. In the end, that option for stakeholder engagement promised to be the most strategically advantageous, giving executives additional options as circumstances evolved in a highly volatile sector for years to come.

Strategic foresight

Finally, political risk can be woven into strategic decisions and broader strategic planning through strategic foresight. As globalization evolves, C-suites and boards will likely want to conduct deeper dives into how the landscape is evolving *even absent some immediate question*—combating what some have termed the "radical uncertainty" of today's age.[122] Strategic foresight is the systematic management of future uncertainty using methodologies designed first to *reduce* the range of future uncertainty and, second, to *structure* the uncertainty that remains.

A whole suite of methodologies has emerged in this realm, but the most useful for executives is scenario planning. While we have already highlighted the utility of scenario analysis in *managing* political risk, *strategists* who employ scenario planning have a different focus—they seek to explore multiple alternative futures to design and test the best path forward for their companies. And they benefit from assessing the dynamics that are likely to affect their future decisions before there is a direct impact from an urgent situation. Because political risk is driven by a complicated set of actors and influences, companies often find it difficult (or, some would argue, impossible) to predict the future—it is, almost by definition, within the realm of "radical uncertainty." That's why exploring different scenarios and identifying which strategic actions can be taken to position a company for the future *today* is so valuable.

To get started with a scenario analysis exercise, a company's strategy team should establish key uncertainties: for example, the team might select a set timeframe for the scenario analysis (e.g., five years out, 10 years out, and so on). The team should then identify the likely drivers of the future environment in that timeframe, assessing those drivers regarding how certain they are and how significant their impact would be on the organization. As a final part of this first step, the team should select two highly impactful and uncertain drivers to be the *key* uncertainties.

Second, the team should develop future scenarios. This is done by conducting research into the two key uncertainties, as well as other drivers identified in the first step, to assess recent trends and different ways in which they might evolve. This second step can involve secondary research, interviews with subject matter experts, analysis of historical case studies, and more. Next, the team should analyze the potential interactions *between* the drivers, developing narratives about how the situation could evolve in each scenario and what the environment would look like at the end of the identified timeframe. As the last part of this step, the team should identify signposts that might suggest to observers which scenario is beginning to play out.

Third, the team should assess the implications of each scenario. This should include consideration of the likely policy responses and second-order effects by the key geopolitical players. Beyond that, the team should consider the implications for the global business environment (see figure 16). How would each scenario play out for the organization through a structured focus analysis?

Finally, the team should identify and prioritize strategic actions the company should take given the intelligence gleaned from these exercises. What could be done *now* to position the company strategically for each future possibility? The team should then prioritize these potential actions by considering questions, such as the following: Which actions are effective across multiple scenarios? That is, which strategic actions provide the company with

FIGURE 16.
POLITICAL RISK SCENARIO ANALYSIS CAN
BE A POWERFUL TOOL FOR STRATEGIC PLANNING

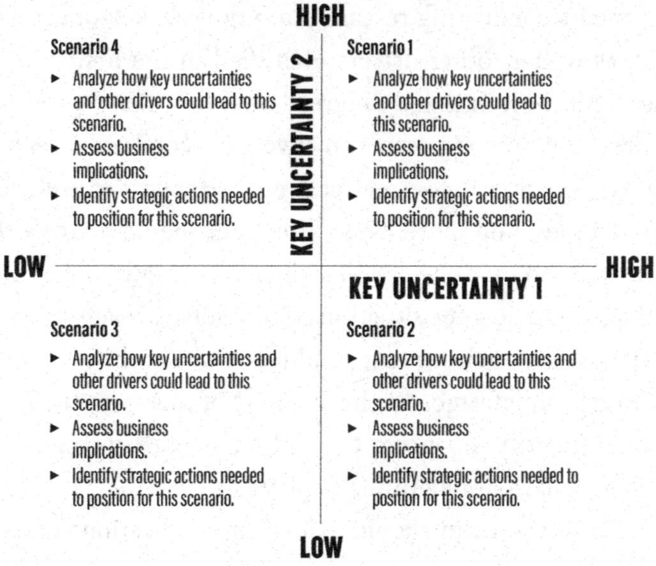

HIGH

Scenario 4
- Analyze how key uncertainties and other drivers could lead to this scenario.
- Assess business implications.
- Identify strategic actions needed to position for this scenario.

Scenario 1
- Analyze how key uncertainties and other drivers could lead to this scenario.
- Assess business implications.
- Identify strategic actions needed to position for this scenario.

KEY UNCERTAINTY 2

LOW ———————————————— **HIGH**

KEY UNCERTAINTY 1

Scenario 3
- Analyze how key uncertainties and other drivers could lead to this scenario.
- Assess business implications.
- Identify strategic actions needed to position for this scenario.

Scenario 2
- Analyze how key uncertainties and other drivers could lead to this scenario.
- Assess business implications.
- Identify strategic actions needed to position for this scenario.

LOW

Source: EY Geostrategic Business Group.

the most geopolitically robust strategy across various scenarios? Which actions are appropriate in the most likely scenario(s)? Which actions would be most impactful in strategically positioning for future growth? Which actions would provide the greatest resilience? And which actions are the least costly or disruptive?

EY teams have employed strategic foresight with a range of companies facing various strategic decision points. One client was considering whether to expand into a particular market. While testing the initiative with a pilot phase that involved opening a small number of locations, the CFO and investment office wanted to glean a better understanding of the ways rising geopolitical tensions might affect the market expansion opportunity and investment thesis.

The company's executives understood that political dynamics around their market of interest were likely to evolve in the next five to 10 years. But they did not have a view as to how exactly that might play out or how it could affect their investment horizon. So, EY teams worked with them to compile a forward-looking scan and a focus-style assessment on how those likely political risks would affect the company's potential market entry. This part of the effort complemented other ones that focused on the market's competitive landscape, domestic demand trends, and a variety of other factors.

EY teams then conducted a scenario analysis that explored how the geopolitical environment appeared most likely to evolve in the next five to 10 years, emphasizing the evolving relationships between the company's home-country government and the government of the market in question. This amounted to a set of more than 10 identified risk areas, each assessed on a four-level spectrum of potential outcomes and with the relative likelihood also assessed. Certain scenarios carried significant risks to the company's continuity of operations, compliance requirements, and revenue prospects in the target market. Some carried significant reputational risks in the company's home market as well. The range was expansive.

Next, EY teams worked with the company to define their "red line" around each identified risk area—that is, the point of escalation at which the negative business impact from the investment would supersede what the company was willing to accept. Separately, a determination was made of the most likely outcome for each risk area on a defined time horizon. Together, the visibility into whether any red lines would be crossed at the individual risk area level then informed the company's overall go or no-go decision on expansion in the market. A "no-go" decision was sure to leave the company with a loss in costs related to the ongoing pilot. Alternatively, the scenarios falling short of the company's red lines presented executives with a series of strategic choices. They could maintain their small footprint, spending millions of dollars every year on a course that would limit the country's exposure. Or executives could double down on the pilot effort and move forward with the market entry—choosing to invest more to expand the company's presence.

By mapping probabilities of the qualitative scenarios envisioned against the known investment-related costs, executives had a much more refined understanding of the true costs associated with pursuing various strategic alternatives. And, even if certain red lines had not already been crossed, getting a clear understanding of what *could* trigger a red line in the future—that is, which warning signs the company could monitor to suggest they were nearing a red line—gave them a better chance of reacting optimally in such a scenario. Having conducted the scenario analysis, the executive team was confident presenting its geopolitically informed recommendation to the board.

EMBRACING A PROACTIVE APPROACH

The trigger points, tools, and stories explored here make clear when and how companies should incorporate political risk into their future-oriented strategies. But many executives, having taken full stock of the effort required to weave political risk into the strategy function, may ask themselves these important questions: Is the investment worth it? Is a company wise to expend the hours and resources required? Does it make sense to develop the just-in-case framework that allows for quick pivots at some guaranteed expense?

Our answer, of course, is yes. To be sure, no one can claim to have a crystal ball—there is no way to ensure that a company can predict with full accuracy how political risk will evolve over any given number of years. Executives can only hope to understand what *may* occur, the likelihood of that change, and what the potential impact may be on their business. Importantly, proactively incorporating political risk into strategy would help to both mitigate downside risks and identify upside opportunities that would otherwise have been missed.

So, what's the upshot? We studied this very question in 2021, looking to understand what the downstream implications were of executives choosing to weave political risk proactively into corporate strategy versus those that chose not to. The aggregate data is presented earlier in this chapter in figure 10, but there are important distinctions. The former group, which we termed "proactive companies," worked to identify, assess, and manage political risks—to prepare for what might happen in the future. "Reactive companies," by contrast, identified, assessed, and managed political risk in a way that presumed they would be able to pivot as changes emerged. So, how did these two groups respond when the global economy was disrupted by government policy responses to an unforeseen crisis? The COVID-19 pandemic provides a useful case.

First, it's important to note that impacts from the pandemic affected companies, sectors, and countries in various ways; not everything can be boiled down simply to a company's approach to political risk. Nevertheless, the disparity between proactive and reactive companies was remarkable and telling: in the aggregate, proactive companies responded to the pandemic by diversifying their supplier bases (a net of 49 percent), curtailing the length of their supply chains (13 percent), and expanding their international footprint (15 percent). They were more open to large M&A deals (15 percent). Therefore, they were more prone to embrace regionalization strategies when various countries moved to implement industrial policies and trade protectionism.

By contrast, reactive companies were more prone to retrench to domestic markets—to try to insulate themselves from the disruptions. They tended to increase domestic M&A (a net of 33 percent) more than international M&A (13 percent), shied away from large M&As (1 percent) and opportunities to enter international markets (–10 percent), and nearshored or onshored their supply chains (16 percent). These defensive strategies appeared like efforts to mitigate risks—and they were. But having a defensive posture, in such a moment of upheaval, meant they were more likely to miss out on strategic opportunities that proactive companies were better equipped to identify and exploit through regionalization. In short, being reactive proved a pretext for being caught on the back foot—and the results had a material impact. Reactive companies were less likely to have experienced revenue growth in the most recent fiscal year than those in the proactive group.[123]

Still, incorporating political risk into strategy is not simple or easy. It takes both effort and tenacity. It depends on the quality of a company's scan, focus, and manage functions. And, to work most effectively, that integration into strategize activities can't be a one-off effort—it needs to be perpetual.

Chief strategy officers (CSOs) and other executives responsible for strategy need to be deliberate about incorporating political risk into their strategic planning because political risks are likely to have a wide range of impacts—both opportunities and challenges—in the coming years. This can include frequent strategic business reviews, identifying and disposing of noncore assets, raising and optimizing capital to fund growth, analyzing capital allocation, managing investors' and stakeholders' expectations, optimizing business models, redesigning core processes to manage disruptions, and increasing investment in building resilient supply chains. Above all, CSOs need to incorporate political risk into strategic planning to better help the leadership team create sustainable, long-term value. In short, CSOs in the new era of globalization must help their companies not only to see around the corner, but also to consider the long-term implications of their short-term strategic choices.

Of course, a CSO, or her or his team, shouldn't execute geostrategy alone. There is an imperative to collaborate with the other executives in charge of scan, focus, and manage. Too often, all of these functions are hindered by the prevalence of siloed units that fail to communicate with one another. To make sure that a company's scan, focus, manage, and strategize functions work well in harmony, companies need to effectively *govern* their geostrategy efforts. And that's where we'll turn next—to the approaches companies can use to ensure that the various elements of any geostrategy effort work seamlessly *together.*

5

GOVERN

Establish a cross-functional geostrategic team

The executives at Unilever had seen it coming before many others. In the early 2000s, the company's competitors, like many major businesses around the world, were incorporating "sustainability" into their marketing plans. Market research revealed that consumers were becoming increasingly drawn to products that boasted having minimal impacts on the natural environment.[124] But in many cases, those assorted efforts were only, well, skin-deep. Efforts to conserve resources or pare back pollution were, in some instances, more like marketing ploys than true transformations of a company's operational approach. And having noticed that broader phenomenon, Unilever's board and executive team decided to do something different. They committed to taking sustainability more seriously—putting it at the heart of their corporate identity and strategy.

The challenge, Unilever realized, was to change the way the company governed its own operations—to alter the way decision-makers framed their decision points and were assigned responsibilities for those decisions. Sustainability needed not only to be addressed through marketing choices— for example, as one-off efforts to anticipate how public attitudes on pollution might affect the popularity of a certain product. It was quite the opposite: Unilever needed to take a more comprehensive approach—one that would weave sustainability throughout the company's wholesale structure, from top to bottom, and from one end to the other. While the company had been tracking its environmental impact since 2000, it opted to do more.[125] And that prompted the company's executives to create what then CEO Paul Polman termed the "Sustainable Living Plan 2010 to 2020."[126]

To guide the effort, the company set very specific aspirations. Over 10 years, executives wanted to halve the environmental footprint of the making and use of their products, eventually setting 70 time-bound targets linked to the United Nations–established Sustainable Development Goals (SDGs).[127] And to make sure those goals were kept front and center throughout the company's organizational chart, executives set up dedicated sustainability-monitoring mechanisms across the company and within senior leadership.[128] The company installed sustainability teams in their finance, R&D, customer development, supply chain, and business operations functions. Each team had a dotted line leading to the chief sustainability officer, who led the global sustainability team. The company also engaged a seven-member sustainability advisory council of outside experts led by the chief R&D officer.[129]

Over the next 10 years, Unilever's Sustainable Living Plan contributed to important changes at the company. At the outset, executives designated seven of the company's top 10 brands, including Dove and Seventh Generation, under a "Sustainable Living Brand" label. Each of those seven brands was tasked, from the get-go, with "identifying and activating" their purpose, which meant not only operating sustainably, but also having a positive social impact.[130] Unilever's Vaseline brand, for example, established skin-healing programs for three million people living in poverty. Through mentoring and career fairs, another brand—Rin—set up a "career academy" for women across rural India.[131] And, in each case, the goal wasn't simply philanthropic. These efforts were done strategically to put the company on a better footing to address sustainability challenges as they arose in the years and decades that followed.

It is impossible to know how Unilever might have fared had it *not* adopted its Sustainability Living Plan in 2010. But the company and, in particular, the brands that were designated under the plan have thrived since its inception. The company's Sustainable Living Brands grew 46 percent faster than the rest of the business in 2017, followed by 69 percent faster growth in 2018—when those brands delivered 75 percent of the company's growth.[132]

It wasn't just revenue growth on which the Sustainability Living Plan delivered; operational costs were lowered as well. Investments in energy-efficient technologies reduced energy consumption and lowered operational costs.[133] Unilever also saved money by proactively reducing its waste footprint by 31 percent, as compared with 2010 levels, through responsible sourcing and supply chain optimization.[134] And by addressing environmental risks, such as water scarcity and climate change, the company reduced its exposure to supply chain disruptions and resource price volatility.[135] Polman's successor, CEO Alan Jope, noted: "We've taken 1.2 billion euros of cost out of the business through sustainable sourcing."[136]

All of this is to say that Unilever was ahead of the curve on sustainability—harnessing the power of organizing corporate governance in support of the company's sustainability goals. And its success proved a beacon. In the years that followed, a whole range of companies began to move past the temptation to use sustainability simply as a marketing strategy, choosing instead to weave ESG more deeply into their governance structures and strategic plans. According to one authoritative count, the number of chief sustainability officers (CSOs) of publicly traded, US-based companies grew sixfold from 2011 to 2023.[137] Momentum has accelerated in recent years, with the number of CSOs jumping from just 44 in 2018 to 183 in 2023. In an EY survey of CEOs of Fortune 1000 companies, every single respondent indicated sustainability and broader ESG issues were important to their company, with 87 percent believing those initiatives are "very" to "extremely" important to their businesses and long-term success.[138] Indeed, in a different recent survey, 70 percent of CSOs said they meet with their CEO fairly regularly—once a month or once a week.[139]

Sustainability is no longer seen as "nice to have" by many companies, but rather an essential pillar of the business. Not only has sustainability emerged as a major focal point for company decision-making across a whole range of industries, sectors, and geographies; it has also emerged as a pillar within corporate governance. Today, we believe that political risk and all the activities laid out in the preceding chapters—Scan, Focus, Manage, and Strategize—need to travel the same road. Geostrategy, like sustainability, needs to move from the periphery to the core of how companies do business. Here, too, some companies are already ahead of the curve. But many face challenges with effective governance of geostrategy.

THE (OFTEN IGNORED) CHALLENGE OF GOVERNANCE

Even companies that are bought into the core dynamic of geo-strategy—those that are eager to embrace the tools that will empower them to scan, focus, manage, and strategize—often overlook governance. And that's not for lack of interest in building a structure around good processes and systems, but because, in some cases, the individual elements of any good process often consume so much attention. In other cases, companies may struggle with inflexible management roles that have yet to adapt to the nature of today's global business environment. In the *Geostrategy in Practice 2021* survey, we found that while governance structures appear to be central to improving political risk management and a company's confidence in its approach, executives do not prioritize investments in this area. In fact, only 14 percent of executives pointed to governance as a key improvement area in political risk management—the lowest of any geostrategy area.[140]

But to make geostrategy work—to build a sustained and effective system for strategically managing political risk—governance is the final key. Scan should not be a "set and forget" activity. Similarly, a focus assessment should not be presumed to remain constant. Rather, because the world is so dynamic, conditions are ever-changing, and new information is perpetually flowing in and out of various units of any company, so the rhythms and channels of information within a company need to be consistently nurtured. And doing that in a smart way means paying much closer attention to how those information flows are *governed*. Who has the information? Who needs it? How will it travel to the place it needs to go in time for decision-makers to weave it into their decision matrices? Put simply, political risk can't be managed without a proper governance system.

Fortunately, there *are* established models for good governance. And to understand how to find the optimal model for a company, it's first helpful to understand the extremes. Later in this chapter, we explore a set of extremes associated with functional teams organized horizontally across the company. But here, we focus on governance extremes in terms of company verticals—headquarters vs. country or regional units.

At one extreme, political risk governance is overly centralized—responsibility for the various elements of a company's geostrategy is put in the hands of a high-level team at a company's headquarters. This approach is based on the presumption that only a central node can pursue a comprehensive vision and action plan. In theory, this governance model resolves the often-cited parable of the blind men and the elephant—a group of blind men who touched different parts of an elephant and came to wildly different conclusions about its overall composition and appearance. Given *all* the information, the experts at headquarters in a centralized system should be able to put news of the trunk, and the legs, and the tail, and the ears together into the full picture of the elephant. This management style is meant to enable C-suite decision-making via a centralized view of global developments.

But however tempting an exclusively centralized approach may be, it creates challenges and blind spots. It's very important to realize that overly centralized geostrategy is prone to miss important context and nuances, some of which are likely to have significant upside or downside impact. In effect, while the central node can see the whole elephant, the component parts may lack the proper scale, or the overall picture may be fuzzy and out of focus. The people on the sales or finance or government relations or supply chain teams may feed information into headquarters that connects to circumstances that aren't easily understood absent a fuller conversation. Connections and context that might seem obvious on the ground in a certain market, or on the factory floor at a certain supplier, might be almost entirely opaque to those at headquarters reading the reports. And, in that confusion, a great deal of intelligence can be lost.

Consider a hypothetical case: local managers identify a particularly important social issue to consumers in a certain market. They make minor adjustments locally, but do not report the issue to the team at headquarters because they have not been asked to provide such intelligence—and they believe the centralized decision-makers won't take it into account in any case. Then, in an offhand remark made at a public forum, the CEO uses rhetoric that appears insensitive to the company's consumers in that one market. While that comment doesn't attract much attention globally, word spreads among consumers in that market and those consumers choose to purchase a competitor's products instead, leading to short-term sales and revenue goal shortfalls in the market and longer-term reputational damage.

That's the problem with overly concentrating political risk management in the center of an organization. But the other extreme can be just as counterproductive. If political risk is handled exclusively at the periphery of an organization—if, for example, risk in Southeast Asia is handled exclusively by the team working in Southeast Asia or if the procurement team handles a risk in isolation from the rest of the functional teams—whatever advantage there was to centralizing the process in the previous scenario is entirely lost. The information gets siloed. No one catches the obvious synergies—or conflicting trends—across regions or functions. As several executives whose companies had adopted this decentralized approach explained to us in qualitative interviews, when issues are managed at a local level, companies lose the benefit of cross-functional insights sharing. When everyone is an expert in only one or two elements of the elephant, no one is entirely confident on how to put all the pieces together.

Consider how this might play out: after a local government pushes for greater onshoring or nearshoring, a company's executives in that market announce that they will explore new manufacturing investments there. But because the announcement was not coordinated with other parts of the company, the local decision-making team does not realize how that investment might reverberate elsewhere. And, as it happens, the government in another large market, angered to see the expansion in the first one, pressures local executives around a similar investment there. As a result, executives at headquarters are blindsided and forced now to review new investments in *both* markets or else manage the political risks (e.g., reputational and compliance) associated with expanding in only one market and reneging on a commitment in another.

While both of these extremes harbor what can be disastrous drawbacks, they each boast something worthwhile. A company *should* want those on the organization's periphery to be engaged in geostrategy—to be aware of what's happening politically in the markets where they operate, and to be thinking perpetually about risks and opportunities there. The same goes for department leaders who have a narrow view of a single business or function. And a company *should* want there to be engagement at the top—for the scan, focus, manage, and strategize functions to be coordinated at the enterprise level across various parts of a company by an executive team. And fortunately, through good governance, companies need not choose between either extreme. They can develop a balance—one that weaves together centralized management and peripheral insights such that a company can glean the best that geostrategy has to offer, while avoiding the pitfalls. Geostrategy can both present clear images of the trunk, legs, tail, and ears, *and* have a clear and comprehensive view of the whole elephant. But it takes good *governance*.

So, how do executives describe their actual governance practices? Fewer than one-quarter of companies conduct any of the political risk governance activities at *both* the enterprise and the functional or business unit levels, according to our research. Instead, around two-thirds of companies rely on governance solely at the enterprise level.[141] And while depending solely on centralized governance may have made sense in a more globalized world, the current global environment demands new rigor.

Of course, for all these examples of how geostrategic governance can go wrong, there are plenty of examples of companies that have figured it out. Many mining companies, for example, operate in very volatile places, even while selling raw materials all around the globe. And many have worked to strike the right balance by investing a great deal of responsibility in the team they have deployed in a single geography—the country team—even while ensuring that those at headquarters are deeply involved. To that end, many have developed governance structures that ensure *shared* responsibility; they maintain massive flows of information between those on the ground and those in the C-suite, including the views of external advisors. And the result is a shared understanding of inherent and residual political risk levels, and a collaborative focus on future strategic success.

A more specific and recent example comes from a company whose board of directors was concerned about a particular set of political tensions escalating into an armed conflict, which would have significant impacts on the company's business. The risk team tasked with exploring this issue didn't try to tackle it on their own. Instead, they put together a multifunctional group of executives from across different geographies to explore the risk and assess different aspects of its potential impacts. The company's collaborative culture and directive from the top ensured that there was no great hurdle to getting everyone to work together to assess and assemble the various components of this particular elephant—everyone felt consulted, and they fully engaged on thinking through the potential challenges and opportunities. The team presented a holistic assessment of the impact of the risk on markets broadly and their company specifically—along with a series of actions that could be taken to manage the risk and some strategic questions for the company's board to consider. In this way, the company was able to benefit from business-line perspectives and a centralized vantage point into focusing, managing, and strategizing around this particular risk.

All of this is to say that governance of political risk matters. How a company establishes and manages the systems that integrate geostrategy into each team's work and ensures that the information is coordinated across teams can have an enormous impact on whether that company's geostrategy succeeds. Beyond simply having the functions and people required to implement a geostrategy, you need the right systems to make the four geostrategy teams—scan, focus, manage, and strategize—work well together. And that means upholding three governance fundamentals: ownership, communication, and trust (see figure 17). *How* to do that is what we'll delve into next.

FIGURE 17.
GOVERN: ESTABLISH A CROSS-FUNCTIONAL GEOSTRATEGIC
TEAM BUILT ON THREE GOVERNANCE FUNDAMENTALS

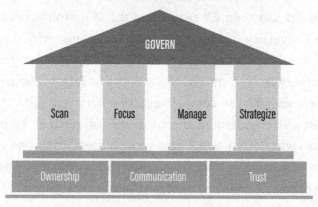

Source: EY Geostrategic Business Group.

A BALANCED APPROACH TO GEOSTRATEGY

So, how can a company establish the most effective governance of political risk? As demonstrated earlier in this chapter, there are adverse impacts of placing too much emphasis on empowering the periphery *or* the center of an organization. The governance structure needs to enable *balance* across company verticals. And just as neither the country teams nor the headquarters should dominate the process, none of the horizontal teams should do so either. That is, none of the core competencies of geostrategy—scan, focus, manage, and strategize—should be allowed to overwhelm the others. Each one of these activities and competencies is crucial. But if any single element of a geostrategy operation gets too much attention, there is a risk that other elements may suffer. And so great governance requires a certain degree of discipline—oversight from above that lets the various elements complement each other while supporting coordination across the geostrategic areas.

This balance can be difficult for many C-suites working to improve their geostrategic capabilities. Joint research between EY teams and the Wharton School of the University of Pennsylvania revealed just why this is frequently so tricky. In a set of executive interviews, most interviewees recognized the benefits of each of the competencies and the complementarity between them. But most also highlighted the trickiness of getting the balance right. Often, rapid growth or leadership in one element threatens to undermine growth and development in the others—leading to underperformance in political risk management overall. The intention should be to ensure that the scan, focus, and manage activities become more balanced, so that they can collectively inform and coordinate with strategy.

For example, if a geostrategy team develops a sophisticated scan function without placing equal weight on the remaining activities, geostrategists will struggle to embed political knowledge in the core business systems and processes. Companies that excel at scan will be able to dynamically identify and monitor political risks. And they're likely to have more and richer data spanning a wide array of quantitative and qualitative sources. But if the focus, manage, and strategize functions are not as fully developed, the scanners' depth of attention paid to changes outside the company will subsume efforts to incorporate that wisdom through financial models, dashboards, and metrics that facilitate coordination across other functions.

As an example, this imbalance recently crystalized for a company that had a key dependency on a person in the government affairs department who owned key relationships with government officials in a material and high-risk market for the business. The company's ability to respond tactically to the external environment was heavily reliant on how this individual engaged with, influenced, and gathered intelligence from key figures in the local and national governments. When this key individual left the business, it created a political risk management challenge. The leadership team had to materially change its approach to managing risk, at pace, in order to maintain line of sight on its key political risks in the region. This included the delineation of roles and a move away from concentrating responsibility on one individual.

Now take another case that relied too much on focus capabilities. Every company, of course, needs the focus function to assess the magnitude of a risk's impact on various business functions. Companies with this capability will understand the specific pathways by which political risks can affect their company—as well as how they can act at the business unit or country level to influence and manage the political risks they face. And, for good reason, that job often falls to more specific business units, where the particular political risk is most material. But pushing too much power to individual functions may tempt business units to resist corporate-level oversight as well as any standardization of data structures and tools. Doing so risks undermining the corporate-level development of political acumen, financial models, and strategic trade-offs. And excessive decentralization can undermine efforts to strengthen communication channels and lower the threshold of what gets communicated across functions and business units.

A company with which EY teams recently worked faced a similar challenge. The company was considering various risk impacts on its operation. But the locus of analysis was pushed almost exclusively to the supply chain team, which, based on its own expertise, was focused primarily on how shifts in the political landscape might affect their ability to acquire the raw materials required to produce the products the company sold around the world. While working with EY teams, the company's risk team, which focused on a whole range of other issues, and its government affairs experts were brought into the process. The company was then able to draw expertise from those with perspectives beyond operational considerations.

Companies that invest too heavily in the manage function run the risk of overlooking the quality of the inputs they're using to make decisions. These companies may be good at incorporating political risk trends into enterprise-wide tracking of risks and implementation of risk mitigation activities. But this often goes hand in hand with political risk being lumped with other macroeconomic risks (e.g., currency or interest rate risk). In doing so, companies leave a suite of potential management actions off the table because the manifestation of some political risks are within the company's control—such as those born from stakeholder relations. The absence of strong linkages between risk managers and their scan and focus counterparts may result in truncated analysis of the relative costs and benefits of alternative risk management strategies that rely more on actions residing in other functions. It may also lead to situations in which central risk managers have made determinations regarding the company's risk profile, but these do not reach the frontline business managers overseeing related decisions on a daily basis.

A company was motivated to rework its approach based on this very challenge. The risk management team was in charge of the risk registry and "owned" the process of analyzing incoming data and intelligence. But the identified risks were generally high level—and the roster of considerations informing the risk management team's analysis was rarely informed by the company's broader scan of relevant political risks. The company's operational team—IT, HR, and others—were not consulted in a systematic way, such that those analyzing risk had only a cursory understanding of how various risks would generally affect the company. And the company's strategy team was also separate, meaning that decisions on strategy were rarely shaped by the company's own risk profile and risk appetite. Recognizing this disconnect, the risk management team began to proactively communicate with these various other functions—which led to a better-informed risk registry and greater visibility on cross-cutting risks.

Finally, while firms are wise to weave political risk into broader efforts to form corporate strategy—risk analysis is key to unearthing opportunities that could provide competitive advantage—an overwhelming investment in strategy can limit a company's political risk management to high-level goals at the expense of day-to-day operations. In some cases, this hyper-focus on the future can lead the company to discount the political risks that are already affecting the business in the present.

One example of an overreliance on the strategy in geostrategy comes from a company that gave its strategy team de facto responsibility for political risk because executives wanted it at the corporate strategy level. But the strategy team didn't think they had the necessary expertise to scan, focus, or manage political risk, so they sought help from other teams within the company. Although this made sense in theory, no other teams felt responsible or accountable for political risk, so they often did not feel compelled to proactively flag the concerns and share them with those who had overall responsibility—which meant the strategy team didn't have the insights needed to set political risk-resilient strategic plans.

All of this is to argue not that any single function of political risk management is more important than the others—they are *all* crucial. For that reason, balance needs to be maintained. However, our research finds that more than half of executives say their company takes an unbalanced approach to political risk management, meaning they are overweight or underweight in certain competencies.[142] The most overweight area is scanning to understand the political risk environment. This means that while companies are investing in gleaning political risk insights, this analysis is likely not filtering through in the most effective way to manage and strategize activities (which are relatively underweight). And the most underweight competency is the operational expertise associated with focus activities—which may be related to the fact that it is seen as the most challenging aspect of geostrategy. The goal of any additional investment in geostrategy should be to target the competencies in which a company is currently underweight so that scan, focus, manage, and strategize expertise and activities become more balanced, promoting more proactive and strategic political risk management.

BUILDING THE GEOSTRATEGIC INFRASTRUCTURE

With the intention of pursuing a balanced approach to geostrategy, executives first need to identify the roles that should be involved in the governance of this process. And they need to find the right people—with the relevant skills and expertise—to implement their company's geostrategy. In our experience, building this infrastructure is an area where many companies continue to struggle.

The right roles

No real consensus has emerged among executives about which players in any given company should be tasked with responsibility for geostrategy, as executives indicate a wide array of roles are involved (see figure 18).[143] This may show that many companies are experimenting with various ownership structures. And there is also differentiation by sector, where certain industries with historically high cross-border

FIGURE 18.
WHO IS RESPONSIBLE FOR GEOSTRATEGY VARIES ACROSS COMPANIES

Who at the senior management level is responsible for political risk management (either as an individual or part of the relevant function or committee)?

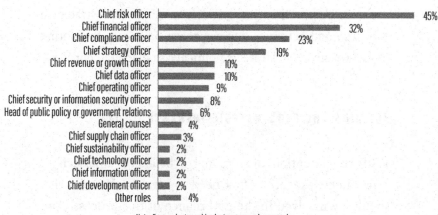

Note: Respondents could select as many roles as apply.
Source: EY Geostrategy in Practice 2021.

activity or government regulation tend to have more sophisticated structures in place. But, explicitly because companies want a wide diversity of people in different roles in the company to be invested in geostrategy, it often makes sense to spread ownership across a variety of different positions.

Most often, responsibility is assigned to the chief risk officer (CRO) or the company's risk function. This is unsurprising given that "risk" is often seen as the operative word in "political risk management." As discussed above, though, political risk should not be automatically assigned to the CRO's portfolio of responsibilities. In many cases, there is a need for a broader set of C-suite executives to be involved in implementing a balanced approach to geostrategy. In addition, some companies may not even have a fully mature risk function or stand-alone CRO role—which is another reason to shift away from automatically allocating political risk to the CRO office.

Interestingly, about one-third of companies seem to task the CFO, or the company's finance or treasury department, with the responsibility for political risk management. One potential reason for the popularity of the CRO and CFO is that responsibility for geostrategy needs to be in a cross-functional office tasked with coordinating strategies for multiple stakeholders within the company; it does not make sense for a more discrete or siloed business function to own it. And it is important for the responsible party to have a voice in the design and implementation of initiatives in the enterprise's key functions, from finance to marketing and R&D. The CROs or CFOs—or, indeed, any individual or function with strategic, cross-functional authority—are therefore natural choices for the coordination of geostrategy.

Unfortunately, in many cases, some of the roles that can add real value to the process are either excluded from geostrategy or fail to engage. Most notably, only 6 percent of executives said the head of public policy, public affairs, or government relations has any responsibility for political risk management. This raises the question of whether companies' geostrategy teams include sufficient political expertise or have the necessary scan inputs to their operational, risk, and strategic models. Without the inclusion of public policy, it is unlikely political risk mitigation and strategic decision-making will be adequately tuned to the right risk exposure. And given the prominent role public affairs teams have in supporting the C-suite in communicating organizational strategy to government, media, and other external stakeholders, not including them in the process presents a potentially sizeable missed opportunity.

Another missing member from many geostrategy teams is the chief operating officer (COO) or chief supply chain officer, as only 12 percent of companies include these roles on their geostrategy teams. Without these executives and their associated teams, how can geostrategists focus on the likely impacts of political risk events? Their exclusion from political risk management responsibilities could help explain why political risk management is so reactive on impact assessments—and why this is the area of political risk management global executives point to as most in need of improvement.[144] Too often, the geostrategy team doesn't include the view of the people best placed to evaluate how potential political risk events would impact a company's operations and supply chain.

The chief strategy officer (CSO) is included in responsibility for political risk management more often than the scan and focus functions, but still only about one-fifth of companies include the CSO in their geostrategy teams.[145] This means that many companies may be less able to position their company's exposure to political risks across the markets in which they choose to play. And without the CSO's perspective influencing geostrategic decisions, the company may view political risks only as challenges to be avoided, rather than also seeking to identify opportunities that could provide competitive advantage in the future. And the CSO often also contributes a perspective oriented toward long-term business objectives critical for geostrategy.

That's why, to do governance right, the buy-in and direction need to come right from the top. Engaging the CEO in geostrategy governance is crucial for ensuring that each of the underlying functions' insights is woven through every element of a company's operation. CEOs should receive a regular assessment of how geopolitical developments and other political risks affect current operations, and also ensure the proactive inclusion of political risk analysis in forward-looking strategic planning, including M&A, market entry and exit, and international footprint decisions. The CEO also has a critical role to play in setting the "tone at the top" as related to political risk, providing top-down guidance on how she or he views the impact of political risk on the business across operational, financial, and strategic decisions.

The board also has an important role to play. In today's volatile geopolitical environment, the minimum requirement for boards is to stay informed about the political risks facing the company and its business environment, and to posit questions to executive management around this topic about its effects on business strategy.[146] In back-to-back years of the EY *Geostrategy in Practice* surveys, executives said that their boards were dedicating additional time to political risk compared with the previous year. But, on average, we have found boards pay the most attention to its impact on *existing* strategy (40 percent); a far lower share (25 percent) consider political risk as part of making *new* business decisions.[147] And the *EY Global Board Risk Survey 2023* (GBRS) identified geopolitical events as one of the top risks that directors expect to have a significant impact on their companies. But only 43 percent of directors said geopolitical risk was part of their governance oversight, which points to a gap in which considerable work should be done.[148]

Of most concern is the fact that fewer than one-quarter of boards regularly receive political risk briefings from external experts or engage in scenario analysis on political risks and the macro environment.[149] A similarly small percentage receive regular briefings by company functions. And only 40 percent of directors say they engage with C-suite executives more than twice a year.[150] Amid heightened geopolitical tensions, there is a recognition that addressing political risk falls within the board's oversight responsibilities. In a more complex and volatile world, directors need to reconsider everything from the timing and mode of meetings to how they gather and scan information to assess which political risks are most material to their companies. Doing so will enable boards to take a more strategic and data-driven approach to improve oversight of one of the most material risks facing their companies.

The right people

Of course, governance isn't just about structure or assigned responsibility. It's also about *people*. Companies need to ensure that they're recruiting the right individuals with the proper credentials, expertise, and talent to build a competent geostrategy function. This can be a challenge, though, because not many people have "geostrategist" on their CV. Rather, just as various company functions need to be involved, strong geostrategy teams need an array of professional experiences, including both political and business acumen.

Many companies look to ex-diplomats, ex-military officials, or political insiders (often affiliated with a particular political party) to glean a stronger understanding of political risk. And this can be worthwhile. Such former officials will usually have interesting and unique insights, ensuring that the company is quicker to identify emerging risks and more readily equipped with advisors capable of bringing sophisticated analysis to developing problems. This category of geostrategists also tends to have deep personal networks among organizations involved in their areas of expertise, providing a useful community in which to test ideas and compare viewpoints.

But three problems may arise when companies rely too heavily on these sorts of individuals. First, few of these individuals have a deep expertise in business, which can make it challenging for them to translate political dynamics into implications for the company or to get the flow of information going to the right places. And such individuals can quickly grow out of touch. Sometimes, their views can become stale as their experience fades into the past and their networks shrink as their friends and contacts retire or lose political power. Moreover, some ex-political officials tend to be exponents of the conventional wisdom, meaning they are unwilling to stray too far off the beaten intellectual path.

Another common approach is to hire people with a background in risk management or with a breadth of operational experiences and knowledge across the company—people often well-versed in ERM, finance, and operational structures. On the upside, these people are often better able to embed risk mitigation into operations and strategic plans, and to elevate political risk into high-level decision-making processes. However, many of these company generalists lack scan experience, so they may fail to recognize the unique developments or trends of political risk events. And they are more likely to lump political risk with macro-level financial risks. As a result, they may truncate analysis of the relative costs and benefits of alternative risk management strategies that rely less on financial tools.

So, there's no perfect profile for those who might lead a company's geostrategy team. Neither an ex-government official nor a longtime operational manager from a company are likely, in isolation, to have all the skills and experience necessary to implement geostrategy. The (perhaps somewhat unsatisfying) answer is that those involved in geostrategy need a mix of skills, backgrounds, and competencies that complement one another. The collection of backgrounds offers an opportunity for diverse perspectives to enable better outcomes. And these individuals need to be incentivized to work together in an ongoing, collaborative way. That means focusing on three governance fundamentals: ownership, communication, and trust.

Three governance fundamentals

Ownership, communication, and trust are essential fundamentals for effective governance of geostrategy. On ownership, primary management of geostrategy should be assigned to a single point person who is credentialed across functions, or, alternatively, ownership could sit with a cross-functional committee. In the EY *Geostrategy in Practice 2021* survey, about 90 percent of global executives said their company coordinates political risk management through a dedicated political risk function or cross-functional team.[151] But this stands in contrast to findings from the EY-Wharton executive interview efforts and work done with EY clients. We suspect this disconnect is born from the fact that only one-third of executives in the survey report that their company does this on a proactive basis—meaning that, in most cases, these teams or committees are only assembled intermittently or in response to a political risk event. Ideally, that should change.

On communication, companies should establish regular, multidirectional information sharing among all functions or activities involved in geostrategy. Political risk governance appears to be siloed in many companies. But having strong communication channels can cut through silos, enhancing shared understandings of how the business holistically is managing political risk. Ideally, executives should communicate regularly about political risks *horizontally* among each other and in both formal, structured ways and in informal settings as well. Leaders should also regularly communicate *vertically* with teams on key political risks and how they are being managed via operational, financial, or strategic changes. Executive commentary serves the purpose of both informing employees and eliciting responses, which could illuminate risks not fully understood prior. Clear communication channels should be set up between the geostrategy leaders and executives with relevant interests. And escalation procedures for political risk reporting to the CEO and board should be well established.

Finally, the governance structure for political risk management should enhance trust across an organization. Key principals in each function should not only know whom to call in other functions, but they should also have strong working relationships with them. These relationships should align employees and teams, not put them in competition. To be successful at geostrategy, a company's senior leadership should be heavily involved. Developing a high degree of trust between the geostrategy function and senior management can help streamline both crisis responses and recognition of new business opportunities. And, regardless of governance structure, companies should seek to develop a risk culture aware of political risks and related business impacts to further build internal trust.

As a cautionary tale, consider the example of a company whose political risk governance lacked *all three* of these fundamentals. In terms of ownership, different country firms assigned responsibility for political risk management to different roles. In some countries, geostrategy was assigned to the legal unit; in others, it was given to the country manager. The result was to diminish the capacity of headquarters to understand who had the responsibility to perform various geostrategy functions across the global enterprise. Moreover, it was often difficult to determine if and how political risks were being managed and whether those making decisions were sufficiently versed in the overall implications of the risks they faced.

The company also experienced a breakdown in communication regarding geostrategy. The global headquarters sent directives to regional and local teams to perform geostrategy, but did not communicate the end goals of the activities nor get involved in their efforts. C-suite executives became overly reliant on the regional teams to proactively feed them information, but did not establish how or when such communication should flow. The result was predictable. The C-suite was essentially left to fly blind, with key political risks essentially unmanaged at the global level due to lack of communication.

And, perhaps most problematically, trust was also lacking. In one instance, the teams situated in two neighboring countries became competitive with one another, each jealously guarding their own intelligence, reluctantly divulging analysis to the regional head, and resisting any regional coordination in the hopes, presumably, that decision-makers at headquarters would invest in their market, rather than the other. The result was a disjointed and uneven approach to geostrategy that exposed the company to unnecessary political risks in some key markets.

ALTERNATIVE GOVERNANCE STRUCTURES

Of course, every company will need to adopt its own governance structure for geostrategy, both because political risk exposure differs across industries and footprints, and because the overall governance structure of every company is unique. That said, there are several ways to structure the governance, and executives will need to determine which is right for their organization. The detailed specifics aren't too prescriptive; what matters most is that the three governance fundamentals remain at the core of the structure. When a company's board and C-suite manage to weave these values into the governance process, the rest is likely to take care of itself.

Companies should consider whether they would do particularly well to establish an explicitly vertical structure, with a geostrategy leader coordinating the efforts of the scan (e.g., public policy or government relations); focus (e.g., operations); manage (e.g., risk management); and strategize (e.g., corporate strategy) teams (see figure 19). This structure favors centralized decision-making, and establishes a mechanism to braid bottom-up analysis and actions from business units through the corporate functions that understand them best. It also works particularly well when there is a clear geostrategy leader, whether that individual is primarily tasked with geostrategy or oversees it as a secondary role. The challenge, however, is to ensure that silos are broken down and information flows comfortably between the various business unit functions and the geostrategy leader. For that reason, this structure works

FIGURE 19.
VERTICAL GOVERNANCE STRUCTURE FOR GEOSTRATEGY

* The geostrategy leader role could be performed by the chief executive officer, by one of the other executive roles on the chart, or even by a stand-alone chief geostrategy officer operating in a coordinating role.
Source: EY Geostrategic Business Group.

best in companies that generally have a more hierarchical culture or those that have too many business units to make a committee structure viable.

Establishing a geostrategy committee comprising corporate-level and business unit leaders is an alternative to an explicit hierarchy (see figure 20). In this structure, there is typically no single geostrategy leader, though a committee chair could act in this role. The flatter, more horizontal committee structure fosters communication across various teams and levels of the company and can serve to build trust and a more general understanding of the broad range of geostrategy among committee members. The lack of hierarchy, however, can lead to difficulties, including delays in decision-making. For that reason, the committee-focused structure works best in companies that have a more collaborative culture and in those with a

FIGURE 20.
COMMITTEE GOVERNANCE STRUCTURE FOR GEOSTRATEGY

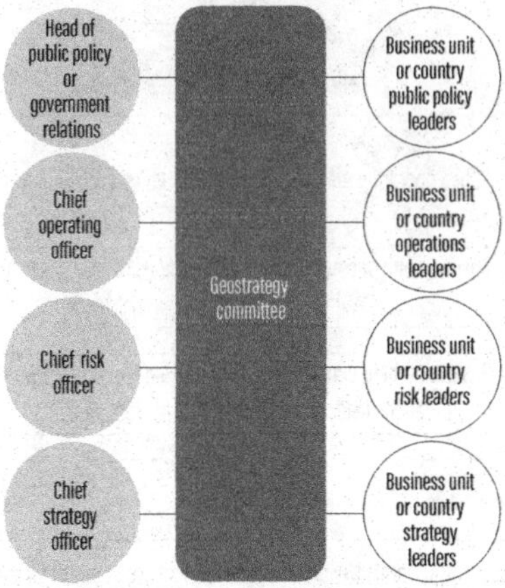

Note: These specific titles may not align with all companies' C-suite structures. The titles are less important than the geostrategy roles they fulfill.
Source: EY Geostrategic Business Group.

smaller number of large business units. It also is a preferred approach when management does not want to develop a stand-alone geostrategy function.

A third alternative is a matrix structure (see figure 21). In this approach, each corporate functional lead liaises with the business unit heads on their respective geostrategy areas. Given that, matrices provide high levels of communication between business units and the corporate level, while also harnessing strong ownership and collaboration at the business unit level. This structure also works well when a company has strong regional or country leadership that seeks to assume responsibility for local political risk considerations, but has limited interests outside of their geography. But the challenge with the matrix is to avoid any turf battles that may develop. And with this approach, business unit leaders need to be "jacks of all trades" when it comes to geostrategy. In the absence of a well-articulated and widely accepted corporate vision, things can go awry.

Regardless of which governance approach a company embraces, the fundamentals need to remain the same. Functions within the geostrategic team that require expertise need to be woven together holistically—individual elements cannot be cut off from the broader team. Individuals and teams from the corporate level and business units need to be involved so that those making strategic business decisions have a full picture. Everyone must buy into the imperative of clear and persistent communication. Everyone involved needs to nurture a sense of trust in the process—and in each other. And each of the individuals involved needs to maintain a sense of ownership over the geostrategic direction of the organization and his or her particular areas of responsibility.

FIGURE 21.
MATRIXED GOVERNANCE STRUCTURE FOR GEOSTRATEGY

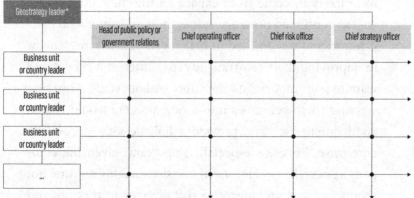

* The geostrategy leader role could be performed by the CEO, by one of the other executive roles on the chart, or even by a stand-alone chief geostrategy officer operating in a coordinating role.
Source: EY Geostrategic Business Group.

WHEN POLITICAL RISK GOVERNANCE SUCCEEDS

A company recently asked EY teams for assistance in the wake of multiple significant setbacks. In markets where the company had significant footprints, political shifts had forced them to make unexpected moves. In one case, for instance, the company was pushed to put on ice an investment that was already underway due to a political risk that materialized. While far from ideal, the company was able to digest the setback. But of more concern to the company's leaders was the reality that they had not anticipated these political shifts—that the company had been forced to meet the changes flat-footed. The executive team was less concerned that the company had made a less-than-fruitful investment—that's unavoidable in business environments full of risk. The worry was that the organization hadn't been prepared. Something needed to change.

Aware that aspects of the company's future growth were likely to come from expansion into new markets, as well as continued presence across their already-global footprint, executives decided to make a substantial investment in improving their geostrategic capabilities. But they didn't want to pour money into the effort without some sense that steering these resources into a new process would return good intelligence and provide a holistic view across the enterprise. This was especially important, given the company's generally decentralized decision-making culture. So, they appointed an enterprise risk director to the role and tasked this individual with overseeing the effort both to get early visibility to emerging political risks and to build a more sophisticated framework and set of processes to account for these external risks. The question was how to do this most expeditiously and effectively.

The company engaged EY teams to help in assessing their maturity in these areas and building tools to broaden the business's capabilities. The team began by carrying out a gap assessment, conducting a review of the company's existing efforts around political risk management and identifying areas that could be strengthened. Next, they bolstered the company's analytical capabilities through designing a customized geopolitical risk response dashboard for regular tracking of key political risk indicators, including both qualitative and quantitative metrics. These included regulatory, trade, macroeconomic, and other factors—traced across each of the company's key markets of operation.

The dashboard was particularly helpful for the company's C-suite. Instead of getting a variety of reports and data points from various teams located in far-flung corners of the globe, executives at headquarters now had one consistent lens through which to understand the political risks affecting the business. But, soon enough, executives realized that the dashboard didn't solve their fundamental geostrategic challenge: the need for effective political risk governance.

Given the strategic nature of this broader challenge, leaders realized that getting everyone who dealt with political risk in the same room was most crucial. In the process of trying to integrate political risk into the ERM system, it had become clear that a whole range of different pockets of geostrategic expertise and activity existed within the company, but they were not communicating with each other systematically. Of even more concern was that they were not incentivized or engaged to coordinate their risk mitigation and management activities with one another. Political risk management was decentralized to such a degree that country units engaged in geostrategy weren't sharing their wisdom or approach with other country units, let alone contributing to a centralized effort at headquarters to develop a more holistic, company-wide approach.

EY teams helped the management team design a standing geostrategic risk committee with the goals of improving communication and coordination of political risk management. Ultimate ownership—and geostrategy committee chairmanship—rested with the ERM leader. But the committee included representatives from strategy, operations, marketing, legal, public affairs, ESG, and HR. It also included product segment leaders and country-level representatives. Importantly, this roster included leaders from both enterprise *and* functional levels, and was sufficiently diverse to harness those representing a range of country and business-unit level members. This, of course, was not an easy ask—it was an extra workload for employees and leaders who were already busy, and meant some leaders would be asked to relinquish sole authority over areas historically managed in silos. But the C-suite stood behind the new structure, so everyone quickly bought in.

As early as their first meeting, committee members saw the value in collectively assessing political risks and learning from each other what mitigating actions were being taken across the company. Trust was fostered. And the committee soon decided to expand its scope to consider other external

risks that the company faced, such as stakeholder expectations around diversity and inclusion efforts. Many of these
other risk areas also had a political component to them—the
company's approach across its various units was sure to play
differently in disparate markets and with various political
actors. And now, with everyone around a virtual table, in
cases where developments were poised to create a risk or
open an opportunity, colleagues knew ahead of time and
could prepare.

Almost immediately, it was clear to the company's leaders that the return on investment was substantial. Various
functions and knowledge hubs of the organization were now
in much better coordination. The new governance structure elevated voices of stakeholders from smaller parts of
the business and enabled committee members to share how
decisions made in other parts of the business affected them.
The process had woven politically driven enterprise risk into
forward-looking strategic considerations.

HOW THIS PLAYS OUT

Some companies today—many of whom came early to the
realization that managing political risk would be of increasing concern as globalization evolved—have already begun
the hard work of building enduring governance structures capable of scanning for risk, focusing on the relevant
impacts, managing likely shifts, and strategizing around
future opportunity. But others, many of whom may view
geopolitical developments and other political risks much as

some viewed sustainability in previous decades, may have erected a less-than-rigorous system as a way to check a box. In these cases, the boards and C-suites may not realize they need to demand and shape a more intentional and professional geostrategic process before catastrophe hits.

We've written this chapter largely as a word of caution and a call to action. Governance, in the end, is the area of political risk management where proactive companies excel relative to other companies. And that's why creating more proactive and cross-functional governance structures for political risk management should be the *first* step toward making improvements across the other areas of political risk management activity. Before trying to scan more effectively or focus more specifically—before trying to improve the way a company manages political risk or develops strategy moving forward—executives should set up a system that weaves all these elements together in an effective way. And that task should be approached in three steps.

Step 1: Create a dedicated function

The first step may seem obvious, but, too often, it's missed: companies must put someone or some entity in charge of shaping the geostrategy governance structure. As many companies realized during the COVID-19 pandemic, the buck must stop somewhere. In order to implement a successful geostrategy, we recommend that companies make an individual, committee, or function ultimately responsible for geostrategy. That executive or body should then be given authority to work cross-functionally with the individuals or teams in charge of the scan, focus, manage, and strategize activities.

Step 2: Assemble the team

What the company should want is for this empowered central node to have the confidence to pull various pockets of expertise together such that they work in harmony. The key is for those leading the effort to build a system capable, as needed, of drawing from multiple areas of expertise. Proactive companies will make sure to include a diverse set of executives in geostrategy governance, including the roles outlined in the governance structures above and potentially also including others, such as the chief data officer, chief security or information security officer, and chief compliance officer. Working together, these executives will be positioned to get ahead of risk—to avoid the trap of being perpetually reactive—by identifying risks, assessing their impact, managing them, and incorporating political risk analysis into strategic decisions, such as M&A transactions.

Step 3: Break down silos

Once the geostrategy team is assembled, those put in positions of responsibility need to use their power to ensure that information is going back and forth everywhere. Those with authority need to avoid becoming wedded to any particular process that might exclude or diminish data coming from any given source, whether it's inside or outside the company. The key, as a coordinating hub, is to maintain intellectual and analytical flexibility. A cross-functional structure will demand data, authority, and respect from the organization as a whole—but that respect needs to run both ways. Those in the farthest corners of the organization need to feel that they benefit from both sending and receiving information and intelligence to and from the central hub. In organizations proactively seeking to manage political risk across the globe, few features could be more important. As stated earlier, it is not enough to simply bring political risk expertise in house—that expertise must be shared broadly across the organization to improve geostrategy. If silos remain, it is almost impossible to enhance understanding about political risks across functions. That is why good governance is so crucial.

CONCLUSION

Seeing the glass as half full

At the beginning of this book, we posed a question: How do executives position a company for growth when the geopolitical future is uncertain? If it holds true that any era of change presents both opportunities and challenges, then it follows that any company has the potential to succeed in uncertain environments. The difference between success and failure often hinges on executives choosing to see the glass as half full, choosing to see and act on the opportunities that volatility and uncertainty present.

The leaders at Toyota were faced with exactly that choice during the world's last moment of significant geopolitical change. The fall of the Berlin Wall and the start of the post–Cold War era of globalization presented companies with a host of new geostrategic decisions in the face of open borders, new markets, and free trade. Rather than simply keep up with the times, Toyota President Shoichiro Toyoda declared that the company must "lead the times" and set a course of ambitious international expansion. Through careful investment informed by geostrategy, Toyota expanded across the globe, doubling its annual overseas production between 1990 and 2000, and becoming a worldwide brand in the decades that followed.

The current period of heightened geopolitical tensions and the evolution of globalization presents executives with a multitude of challenges. But it also presents opportunities to embrace a geostrategy and proactively position for growth in this new era. Whether limiting losses in a fragmenting world or seeking and seizing advantage amid global turbulence, geostrategy will only become more important as we push further into the twenty-first century. As globalization moves into a new era, the importance of geopolitics to corporate strategies is at its highest level in a generation. Geopolitical developments are likely to continue to influence supply chain strategies, shift investment destinations, and push up costs for companies.

To effectively manage and quickly respond to these changes, executives will need to be more attuned than ever to policymakers and their rapidly shifting priorities. Governments are seeking to play a more active role in driving and directing economic activity in their countries, in the pursuit of self-sufficiency and "de-risking." As competing political ideologies and pressures play out, policy volatility will also likely remain elevated. Volatility may be most apparent in abrupt, post-election policy reversals in democratic countries as new leaders shift course away from their predecessors.

Nobel laureate and economist Paul Romer once said that "[a] crisis is a terrible thing to waste." We are *not* in a crisis today (at least not yet). But it *is* an era of significant change—both within the geopolitical system and in policy and regulatory environments in countries around the world—and that is also something executives should not waste. While some tend to see the glass as half empty in terms of heightened levels of political risk that companies face, executives can alternatively choose to see the glass as half full. Forward-thinking business leaders can seize the opportunity associated with today's geopolitical volatility to design and implement a geostrategy to improve political risk management. There are short-term opportunities to be found in mitigating the risks associated with shifts in government policies and geopolitical relations. At the same time, there are also long-term opportunities to seize as companies adjust to whatever new normal arises in the new era of globalization.

EVERY COMPANY NEEDS A GEOSTRATEGY

Finding the opportunities amid today's geopolitical tension requires not just a "glass half full" mentality, but also a willingness to embed geostrategy in how companies do business and set their strategies. In the post–Cold War era of liberalizing economies and expanding global ties, executives were not expected to actively manage systemic geopolitical risks. But today, this is an expectation and a necessity—and it will continue to be in the future. C-suites' ability to embrace these new expectations, challenges, and opportunities will determine which executives lead their companies into successful futures—and which get left behind.

This all begins at the very top: we discussed potential roles of various executives throughout this book, but ultimately it is the CEO's responsibility to set the company up for geostrategic success. As we've outlined in this book, an effective geostrategy requires four distinct activities—and a governance structure that weaves them together (see figure 22).

First, companies must **scan**, identifying and dynamically monitoring geopolitical, country, regulatory, and societal risks. This requires an investment in improved identification and dynamic monitoring of political risks to enhance executives' understanding of the geopolitical environment. Political risks should be included as part of a company's risk identification processes—and tracked through both qualitative and quantitative indicators and analysis.

Second, companies must **focus** that analysis, assessing how these risks could affect the company. This requires impact assessments at the functional and business unit levels, feeding up into an enterprise-wide assessment. In parallel, executives should conduct a top-down assessment at the

FIGURE 22.
THE EY GEOSTRATEGY FRAMEWORK FOR STRATEGIC POLITICAL RISK MANAGEMENT

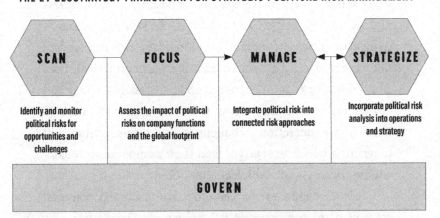

Source: EY Geostrategic Business Group.

corporate level. Companies can model the impact of potential geopolitical developments and other political risk events across key business functions, such as sales, supply chain, investment, and data management.

Third, companies must **manage** the political risks that are most material to their business, integrating them into connected risk approaches for a more holistic view. Such integration can be particularly useful if it leverages the risk identification outputs from the scan processes alongside the tangible estimations of risk impact developed through the focus processes. The risk team responsible for political risk should target hedging strategies that help minimize the impact of downside geopolitical developments and other political risk events, while also proactively identifying strategic opportunities the company could pursue related to upside risks.

Fourth, executives must **strategize** by incorporating geopolitical considerations and other political risk analysis into strategic decisions. Executives should task the geostrategic team with conducting a global footprint assessment for geopolitical risks—and then adjust their footprint strategy accordingly. They should also proactively include political risk analysis in strategic planning processes, especially when pursuing transactions, entering and exiting markets, or refreshing or creating a business strategy.

Finally, and perhaps most importantly, companies must **govern** via a cross-functional geostrategic team. Boards and C-suites need to put in place the proper governance structure so that all of these activities are coordinated across functions and business units. Only in doing so can executives create the culture shifts necessary for the successful integration of geostrategy into business operations and strategy. The specific governance structure is less important than incorporating the three key governance fundamentals: ownership, communication, and trust. The CEO should be actively involved in these processes to demonstrate that there is buy-in from the top on the importance of incorporating political risk into company culture and strategic decisions.

Once the responsibility and structure are established, good governance means establishing the right culture. Political risk should be embedded across an organization. Executives need to be brought in early so they are part of this journey—and so they recognize the benefits to the business of investing in these capabilities. But leaders from (at least) middle management and up also need to buy in to the importance and materiality of political risk to the business. To get this done, geostrategists need to act as internal consultants within the organization—advising colleagues from all parts of the business on the impact of political risk.

Companies that do this successfully will migrate political risk from the periphery to the core, improving their enterprise's resilience to today's challenges and to whatever geopolitical tensions or other political risks may arise in the future. The key here is to avoid the trap of making geostrategy a program where various stakeholders in a company feel as though they are compelled to contribute to the system but get nothing in return. By providing useful information to colleagues, the geostrategic function can and should unlock reciprocal information sharing—gaining critical insight into emerging risk areas throughout the business. Building such interactions can further cultivate a culture of collaboration. Executives can also consider using firm communications and training requirements to further build a culture aware of how political risks affect day-to-day business operations and long-term strategy.

GEOSTRATEGY IS A PROCESS, NOT A PRODUCT

To thrive in an era of geopolitical volatility and uncertainty, companies will need to develop more strategic approaches to managing political risk. The approaches covered in this book are meant to be evergreen. While the challenges may evolve, the methodologies covered here should remain a constant. By embedding geopolitical analysis into a company's DNA, executives will enable their companies to better account for political risks when making strategic decisions, giving them an advantage over competitors in a turbulent geopolitical environment.

Even as companies take these actions, executives need to keep in mind that geostrategy is a process, not a product. Each of the four functional pillars will need constant nourishment and refinement. Geostrategy is never "done." It needs to become a part of how companies understand their external operating environment, manage risks, and design strategies.

The question we get asked most often is centered around what might happen next: What new geopolitical crisis will emerge in the next few years to throw our already-uncertain world into further volatility? Indeed, it is unclear how far many of today's trends will go. How much longer will de-risking remain central to government policymaking, and therefore business strategies? What will be the end result of the primacy of national security concerns on the cross-border flows of labor, capital, products, ideas, and technology? Will other large-scale conflicts emerge to throw whole countries and regions into chaos? We need only look at the recent events in Ukraine and the Middle East as a reminder that geopolitical conflict is possible at any moment.

But whatever the answers may be to these complicated questions about the future, the more important question that executives should ask is how they can set up their companies to properly manage and respond to political risks, both now and in the future. Do we have an effective strategy to manage political risk exposure and seize potential opportunities? With the right geostrategy systems in place, executives will be better equipped to navigate volatility and uncertainty—no matter what specific events occur in the coming years. By implementing the geostrategy framework and creating a culture that embraces geostrategy as an ongoing process, companies can focus on generating competitive advantage, growth, and long-term value.

We hope this book helped provide a lens into how this can be achieved.

ACKNOWLEDGMENTS

This book is the product of the collective knowledge of many colleagues across our respective organizations, and we could not have produced it without their support.

We'd like to thank the entire EY Geostrategic Business Group team, current and former, for sharing their knowledge and experiences with us, both during the development of this book and every day. We'd like to extend a huge thanks to Adam Barbina, Douglas Bell, Alessandro Faini, David Kirsch, Nobuko Kobayashi, Takeshi Konomi, Famke Krumbmüller, Kyle Lawless, Angelika Goliger, Mary Guo, Ari Ben Saks Gonzalez, Jon Shames, and Jay Young. A special thanks goes out to Mary Cline for her encouragement to get this project off the ground and for her moral support along the way. And we'd like to especially recognize and thank Ben-Ari Boukai for all the outstanding efforts that he put into this book, including helping us shape our arguments, identifying company case studies, and generally making sure all our ducks were in a row.

The research team at the Environmental, Social, and Governance (ESG) Initiative at the Wharton School at the University of Pennsylvania were also instrumental in the development of this book. In particular, we'd like to thank Rakhimov Abdurakhim, Christopher Bruno, and Anastasia Gracheva for all their research on political risk and corporate performance, which underpins much of the analysis in this book. Brian Ganson, Tony He, Anne Jamison, and Maithili Kamble also contributed valuable insights in developing new theoretical arguments and data structures that will allow us to build on, further test, and extend the book's arguments going forward.

We'd also like to thank several other people for their research support at various stages of the development of this book: Chandra Bhushan Singh, Kyle Madura, Sumit Mahendru, Viddhi Rohit Parekh, Karan Saksena, Smit Tilak Shah, and Anjali Velu.

This book went through many iterations on its journey to completion. Thank you to Marc Dunkelman for his help in crafting our message in a way that even non-geostrategists can understand—and for sticking with us through many twists and turns. And thank you to Douglas Bell, Liz Bolshaw, and Junko Kaji for providing sage guidance on how to refine our arguments throughout this book. We'd also like to thank Tonny Decker, Megan Duggan, Andrew Hearn, Sally Jones, Shawn Maher, Sharon Sutherland, and John van Rossen for their help in refining certain chapters. Many thanks also go to the dozens of EY colleagues around the world who contributed to and reviewed the client case studies and examples.

Thanks also go to Brooke Maddaford, Suresh Rajan G, Tony Kurian Abraham, and their respective teams for polishing the contents of this book so that it was fit for publication.

Writing this book was only one part of the effort—getting it into the hands of our readers was another. We'd like to thank Emma Davis, Emily Hemming, Nicki Gates, Janet Potter, Laura Williams, and everyone else who helped make sure you knew this book exists.

We'd also like to thank several other individuals who helped in various ways to make this book a reality: Rachael Balls, Linda Cunningham, Ankit Dora, Monika Garg, Douglas Gledhill, Urvi Majhi, Rhea Dutta Majumdar, Katie Meadows, Divya Mohanan, Jayata Sharma, John Shumadine, and Spandana Vakkanti.

Finally, a huge thank you to Kris Pauls for her guidance and support—and the occasional prodding!—throughout this entire project.

ENDNOTES

1   "Overseas Production," Toyota Global website, accessed 15 September 2023.
    https://www.toyota-global.com/company/history_of_toyota/75years/data
    /automotive_business/production/production/overseas/index.html.

2   Atsumi, Toshihiro, "A review of Japanese voluntary export restraint (VER) on
    automobiles," The papers and proceedings of economics 154: 85–96, 31 July
    2017. https://cir.nii.ac.jp/crid/1050845764152697472.

3   "Establishment of the Guiding Principles at Toyota, Toyota Motor Corpora-
    tion," Toyota Global website, accessed 15 September 2023. https://www
    .toyota-global.com/company/history_of_toyota/75years/text/leaping
    _forward_as_a_global_corporation/chapter3/section3/item1.html.

4   "Overseas Production," Toyota Global website, accessed 15 September 2023.
    https://www.toyota-global.com/company/history_of_toyota/75years/data
    /automotive_business/production/production/overseas/index.html.

5   "Sales Volume Overseas," Toyota Global website, accessed 15 September
    2023. https://www.toyota-global.com/company/history_of_toyota/75years
    /data/automotive_business/sales/sales_volume/overseas/region.html.

6   Piketty, Thomas, Capital in the Twenty-First Century (Harvard University
    Press, 2017).

7   Wolf, Martin, The Crisis of Democratic Capitalism (Penguin Publishing
    Group, 2023).

8   World Economic Outlook: A Rocky Recovery, International Monetary Fund,
    April 2023. https://www.imf.org/en/Publications/WEO/Issues/2023/04/11
    /world-economic-outlook-april-2023.

9   Mineral Commodity Summaries (Nickel), US Geological Survey, January 2021.
    https://pubs.usgs.gov/periodicals/mcs2021/mcs2021-nickel.pdf.

10 Mineral Commodity Summaries (Cobalt), US Geological Survey, January 2021.
    https://pubs.usgs.gov/periodicals/mcs2021/mcs2021-cobalt.pdf.

11 Tabuchi, Hiroko, "Before Invasion, Ukraine's Lithium Wealth Was Drawing
    Global Attention," The New York Times, 02 March 2022. https://www.nytimes
    .com/2022/03/02/climate/ukraine-lithium.html.

12 "Global Dynamics," Global Trade Alert, accessed 3 August 2023. https://www
    .globaltradealert.org/global_dynamics.

13 *Political risk and corporate performance: mapping impact*, EYGM Limited, 2019. https://assets.ey.com/content/dam/ey-sites/ey-com/en_gl/topics/geostrategy /ey-political-risk-and-corporate-performance-mapping-impact-final.pdf.

14 Jain, Subhash C., and Grosse Robert, "Impact of Terrorism and Security Measures on Global Business Transactions: Some International Business Guidelines," *Journal of Transnational Management*, March 2009. https://www .researchgate.net/publication/238318597_Impact_of_Terrorism_and_Security _Measures_on_Global_Business_Transactions_Some_International _Business_Guidelines.

15 Harvey, Campbell R., "Country Risk Components, the Cost of Capital, and Returns in Emerging Markets," *SSRN Electronic Journal*: 1–40, 18 November 2004. https://papers.ssrn.com/sol3/papers.cfm?abstract_id=620710.

16 *Geostrategy in Practice 2021*, EYGM Limited, 2021. https://assets.ey.com /content/dam/ey-sites/ey-com/en_gl/topics/geostrategy/ey-ceo-imperative -geostrategy-in-practice-2021.pdf.

17 Lava Jato Case Results, Brazilian Public Finance Ministry (MPF), accessed 24 September 2023. https://www.mpf.mp.br/grandes-casos/lava-jato /resultados.

18 The Editors of Encyclopedia Britannica, "Arab Spring: pro-democracy protest," Britannica, 20 August 2023. https://www.britannica.com/event /Arab-Spring.

19 *Populists in Power Around the World*, Tony Blair Institute for Global Change, November 2018. https://www.institute.global/insights /geopolitics-and-security/populists-power-around-world.

20 *Geostrategy in Practice 2020*, EYGM Limited, 2020. https://assets.ey.com /content/dam/ey-sites/ey-com/en_gl/topics/geostrategy/geostrategy-pdf /ey-geostrategy-in-practice-2020-v1.pdf.

21 *Riding the storm: Billionaires insights 2020*, UBS and PwC, September 2020. https://www.ubs.com/content/dam/static/noindex/wealth-management /ubs-billionaires-report-2020-spread.pdf.

22 "Addressing Economic and Social Council Integration Segment, Under-Secretary-General Says Fair, Equitable Access to COVID-19 Vaccines of Utmost Urgency," United Nations, 02 July 2021. https://press.un.org /en/2021/ecosoc7052.doc.htm.

23 *Geostrategy in Practice 2021*, EYGM Limited, 2021. https://assets.ey.com /content/dam/ey-sites/ey-com/en_gl/topics/geostrategy/ey-ceo-imperative -geostrategy-in-practice-2021.pdf.

24 *Geostrategy in Practice 2021*, EYGM Limited, 2021. https://assets.ey.com
/content/dam/ey-sites/ey-com/en_gl/topics/geostrategy/ey-ceo-imperative
-geostrategy-in-practice-2021.pdf.

25 *Pharma supply chains of the future*, EYGM Limited, 2022. https://assets
.ey.com/content/dam/ey-sites/ey-com/en_gl/topics/life-sciences/life
-sciences-pdfs/ey-pharma-supply-chains-of-the-future-final.pdf.

26 Abnett, Kate, and Jessop Simon, "EU lawmakers move to reject
green gas and nuclear investment rules," Reuters, 30 March 2022.
https://www.reuters.com/business/sustainable-business/eu-lawmakers
-move-reject-green-gas-nuclear-investment-rules-2022-03-30/.

27 *EU taxonomy: Complementary Climate Delegated Act to accelerate decarboniza-
tion,* European Commission, 02 February 2022. https://finance.ec.europa
.eu/publications/eu-taxonomy-complementary-climate-delegated-act
-accelerate-decarbonisation_en.

28 Ganson, Brian, Witold Henisz, and Anne Jamison, "Business & Conflict
Barometer," Africa Centre for Dispute Settlement & Wharton Political Risk
Lab, September 2020. https://esg.wharton.upenn.edu/wp-content
/uploads/2022/07/The-Business-Conflict-Barometer.pdf.

29 Walker, Nigel, "Brexit timeline: events leading to the UK's exit from the European
Union," House of Commons Library, 06 January 2021. https://researchbriefings
.files.parliament.uk/documents/CBP-7960/CBP-7960.pdf.

30 "International Transactions, International Services, and International Investment Position Tables," Bureau of Economic Analysis, 06 July 2023. https://
apps.bea.gov/iTable/?reqid=62&step=9&isuri=1&product=4#eyJhcHBp
ZCI6NjIsInN0ZXBzIjpbMSw5LDZdLCJkYXRhIjpbWyJwcm9kdWN0Iiwi
NCJdLFsiVGFibGVMaXN0IiwiMjQ1Il1dfQ==.

31 "The UK: A top destination for financial and professional services
investment," City of London, April 2023. https://www.theglobalcity.uk
/PositiveWebsite/media/Research-reports/UK-FPS-investment.pdf.

32 "US Market Update," Lloyd's of London, 19 August 2022. https://www.lloyds
.com/news-and-insights/news/us-market-update-2022.

33 "Global insurance premiums," Organization for Economic Cooperation and
Development, accessed 9 October 2023. https://data.oecd.org/insurance
/gross-insurance-premiums.htm.

34 *Geostrategy in Practice 2021,* EYGM Limited, 2021. https://assets.ey.com
/content/dam/ey-sites/ey-com/en_gl/topics/geostrategy/ey-ceo-imperative
-geostrategy-in-practice-2021.pdf.

35 *Geostrategy in Practice 2021*, EYGM Limited, 2021. https://assets.ey.com
    /content/dam/ey-sites/ey-com/en_gl/topics/geostrategy/ey-ceo-imperative
    -geostrategy-in-practice-2021.pdf.

36 "Corporate sustainability due diligence," European Commission.
    https://commission.europa.eu/business-economy-euro/doing-business
    -eu/corporate-sustainability-due-diligence_en.

37 "Business Relationship Economic and Threat Analysis (BRETA),"
    EY website. https://www.ey.com/en_gl/government-public-sector
    /business-relationship-economic-threat-analysis.

38 *Geostrategy in Practice 2021*, EYGM Limited, 2021. https://assets.ey.com
    /content/dam/ey-sites/ey-com/en_gl/topics/geostrategy/ey-ceo-imperative
    -geostrategy-in-practice-2021.pdf.

39 *American Spirits Exports in 2021*, Distilled Spirits Council of the United States,
    March 2022. https://www.distilledspirits.org/wp-content/uploads/2022/03
    /FINAL-DISCUS-2021-Export-Report-March-2-2022.pdf.

40 Voth, Hans-J., and Vasilia Fouka, "Reprisals Remembered: German-Greek
    Conflict and Car Sales during the Euro Crisis," *CEPR Discussion Paper No.
    9704*, October 2013, via Econpapers. https://econpapers.repec.org/paper
    /cprceprdp/9704.htm.

41 Le, Anh-Tuan, and Thao P. Tran, "Does geopolitical risk matter for corporate
    investment? Evidence from emerging countries in Asia," *Journal of Multina-
    tional Financial Management* 62, 100703, December 2021. https://doi
    .org/10.1016/j.mulfin.2021.100703.

42 Blair, G., D. Christensen, and V. Wirtschafter, "How Does Armed Conflict Shape
    Investment? Evidence from the Mining Sector," *The Journal of Politics* 84, no. 1,
    January 2022. https://www.journals.uchicago.edu/doi/abs/10.1086/715255.

43 Dai, L., L. Eden, and P. Beamish, "Place, space, and geographical exposure:
    Foreign subsidiary survival in conflict zones," *Journal of International Business
    Studies*, no. 44, April 2013. https://doi.org/10.1057/JIBS.2013.12.

44 Lin, Leming, A. Mihov, L. Sanz, and D. Stoyanova, "Property rights institu-
    tions, foreign investment, and the valuation of multinational firms," *Journal
    of Financial Economics* 134, no. 1: 214–235, October 2019. https://www
    .sciencedirect.com/science/article/abs/pii/S0304405X19300558.

45 Hasija, D., R.S. Liou, and A. Ellstrand, "Navigating the New Normal: Political
    Affinity and Multinationals' Post-Acquisition Performance," *Journal of
    Management Studies* 57, no. 3, December 2019. https://onlinelibrary
    .wiley.com/doi/abs/10.1111/joms.12545.

46 Henisz, Witold J., and Andrew Delios, "Information or Influence? The Benefits of Experience for Managing Political Uncertainty," *Strategic Organization* 2, no. 4: 389–421, 2004. https://journals.sagepub.com/doi /abs/10.1177/1476127004047619.

47 Holburn, Guy L. F., and Bennet A. Zelner, "Political capabilities, policy risk, and international investment strategy: evidence from the global electric power generation industry," *Strategic Management Journal* 31, no. 12: 1290–1315, 07 April 2010. https://onlinelibrary.wiley.com/doi/abs/10.1002/smj.860.

48 "POSCO Holdings takes the first step in the nickel business for secondary bat-teries in Indonesia," POSCO Newsroom, 28 March 2023. https://newsroom .posco.com/en/posco-holdings-takes-the-first-step-in-the-nickel-business -for-secondary-batteries-in-indonesia/.

49 *2023 Geostrategic Outlook*, EYGM Limited, 2022. https://www.ey.com/en_gl /geostrategy/how-to-shift-strategy-for-a-new-geostrategic-era-in-2023.

50 Carter, David B., and Paul Poast, "Barriers to Trade: How Border Walls Affect Trade Relations," *International Organization* 74, no. 1: 165–185, 23 December 2019. https://www.cambridge.org/core/journals/international-organization /article/abs/barriers-to-trade-how-border-walls-affect-trade-relations /E9D17E0A62C5FB20F348B392FA9C50DB.

51 *Geostrategy in Practice 2021*, EYGM Limited, 2021. https://www.ey.com/en_gl /geostrategy/the-ceo-imperative-are-you-making-political-risk-a-strategic-priority.

52 "Is the AI buzz creating too much noise for CEO's to cut through?" *EY CEO Outlook Pulse Survey July 2023*, EYGM Limited, 2023. https://www.ey.com /en_gl/ceo/ceo-outlook-global-report.

53 Davis, Christina L., Andreas Fuchs, and Kristina Johnson, "State control and the effects of foreign relations on bilateral trade," *Journal of Conflict Resolution* 63, no. 2: 405–438, 23 November 2017. https://journals.sagepub.com/doi /abs/10.1177/0022002717739087.

54 Emont, Jon, "As China Risks Grow, Manufacturers Seek Plan B—and C and D," *Wall Street Journal*, 2 June 2023. https://www.wsj.com/world/china /as-china-risks-grow-manufacturers-seek-plan-b-and-c-and-d-aad7c47b.

55 Wen, Philip, Vibhuti Agarwal, and Greg Ip, "China Finally Has a Rival as the World's Factory Floor," *Wall Street Journal*, 9 May 2023. https://www.wsj .com/world/india-china-factory-manufacturing-24a4e3fe.

56 "Comprehensive and Progressive Agreement for Trans-Pacific Partnership text and resources," New Zealand Foreign Affairs and Trade. https://www.mfat.govt.nz/en/trade/free-trade-agreements /free-trade-agreements-in-force/cptpp/comprehensive-and-progressive -agreement-for-trans-pacific-partnership-text-and-resources/.

57 "Trade Statistics," Japanese Ministry of Finance, accessed 26 July 2023. https:// www.customs.go.jp/toukei/shinbun/trade-st_e/2019/201925ee.xml#pg2.

58 "Trade Statistics of Japan," Japanese Ministry of Finance, accessed 10 January 2024. https://www.customs.go.jp/toukei/srch/indexe.htm?M=23&P=0.

59 *What Do CPTPP Member Country Businesses Think about the CPTPP?*, Center for Strategic & International Studies, August 2021. https://www.csis.org /analysis/what-do-cptpp-member-country-businesses-think-about-cptpp.

60 "FY 2022 Survey on the International Operations of Japanese Firms," Japanese External Trade Organization (JETRO), March 2023. https://www.jetro.go.jp /ext_images/en/reports/survey/pdf/jafirms2022.pdf.

61 Henisz, Witold J., and Jeffrey T. Macher, "Firm- and Country-Level Trade-Offs and Contingencies in the Evaluation of Foreign Investment: The Semiconductor Industry, 1994–2002," *Organization Science* 15, no. 5, 01 October 2004. https://pubsonline.informs.org/doi/abs/10.1287/orsc.1040.0091.

62 "Microsoft announces $1.5 billion investment plan to accelerate digital transformation in Italy, including its first cloud datacenter region," Microsoft Corp., 08 May 2020. https://news.microsoft.com/europe/2020/05/08 /microsoft-announces-1-5-billion-investment-plan-to-accelerate-digital -transformation-in-italy-including-its-first-cloud-datacenter-region/.

63 "EMBRAPII joins the fight against coronavirus," Brazilian Company of Research and Industrial Innovation, accessed 17 July 2023. https://embrapii.org.br/en/.

64 Glennon, Britta, "How Do Restrictions on High-Skilled Immigration Affect Offshoring? Evidence from the H-1B Program," National Bureau of Economic Research, Working Paper 27538, 15 February 2023. https://www.nber.org /papers/w27538.

65 Hassan, Tarek A., S. Hollander, L. van Lent, and A. Talhoun, "Firm-Level Political Risk: Measurement and Effects," *The Quarterly Journal of Economics* 134, no. 4: 2135–2202, 26 August 2019. https://academic.oup.com/qje /article-abstract/134/4/2135/5531768.

66 *VDA Annual Report 2022: Topics and Figures on the Development of the German Automotive Industry*, German Association of Automotive Manufacturing (VDA), November 2022. https://www.vda.de/dam/jcr:b1979803-eb5f-422e-b10f-fa19b374fb80/VDA_5733_JB_2022_EN_WEB_RZ.pdf.

67 Getz, Kathleen A., and Jennifer Oetzel, "MNE Strategic Intervention in Violent Conflict: Variations Based on Conflict Characteristics," *Journal of Business Ethics* 89, no. 4: 375–386, 03 February 2010. https://link.springer.com/article/10.1007/s10551-010-0412-6.

68 Oetzel, Jennifer, Kathleen A. Getz, and Stephen Ladek, "The Role of Multinational Enterprises in Responding to Violent Conflict: A Conceptual Model and Framework for Research," *American Business Law Journal* 44, no. 2: 331–358, May 2007. https://link.springer.com/article/10.1007/s10551-010-0412-6.

69 Xu, Zhaoxia, "Economic policy uncertainty, cost of capital, and corporate innovation," *Journal of Banking & Finance* 111, 105698, February 2020. https://www.sciencedirect.com/science/article/abs/pii/S0378426619302729.

70 Harvey, Campbell R., "Country Risk Components, the Cost of Capital, and Returns in Emerging Markets," *SSRN Electronic Journal*: 1–40, 18 November 2004. https://papers.ssrn.com/sol3/papers.cfm?abstract_id=620710.

71 Desbordes, Rodolphe, "Global And Diplomatic Political Risks And Foreign Direct Investment," *Economics and Politics* 22, no. 1: 92–125, 25 January 2010. https://onlinelibrary.wiley.com/doi/abs/10.1111/j.1468-0343.2009.00353.x.

72 *Economic Impact of Section 232 and 301 Tariffs on U.S. Industries*, United States International Trade Commission, March 2023. https://www.usitc.gov/publications/332/pub5405.pdf.

73 Brogaard, Jonathan, Lili Dai, Phong T. H. Ngo, and Bohui Zhang, "Global political uncertainty and asset prices," *The Review of Financial Studies* 33, no. 4: 1737–1780, 6 August 2019. https://academic.oup.com/rfs/article-abstract/33/4/1737/5544267.

74 *Geostrategy in Practice 2021*, EYGM Limited, 2021. https://www.ey.com/en_gl/geostrategy/the-ceo-imperative-are-you-making-political-risk-a-strategic-priority.

75 EC Article 29 Data Protection Working Party, Guidelines on Data Protection Officers (DPOs), European Commission, 30 October 2017. https://ec.europa.eu/newsroom/article29/items/612048.

76 "More than 100,000 organizations already have a data protection officer," Agencia Española Protección Datos (AEDP), 10 January 2023. https://www.aepd.es/es/prensa-y-comunicacion/notas-de-prensa/mas-de-100.000-organizaciones-ya-cuentan-con-un-delegado-de.

77 Bartley, Tim, and Curtis Child, "Movements, Markets and Fields: The Effects of Anti-Sweatshop Campaigns on U.S. Firms, 1993–2000," *Social Forces* 90, no. 2: 425–451, December 2011. https://academic.oup.com/sf/article-abstract/90/2/425/2235786.

78 McDonnell, M. H., and J. Adam Cobb, "Take a Stand or Keep Your Seat: Board Turnover after Social Movement Boycotts," *Academy of Management Journal*, 24 August 2020. https://journals.aom.org/doi/abs/10.5465/amj.2017.0890.

79 Odziemkowska, Kate, and Witold J. Henisz, "Webs of Influence: Secondary Stakeholder Actions and Cross-National Corporate Social Performance," *Organization Science* 32, no. 1, 27 March 2020. https://pubsonline.informs.org/doi/abs/10.1287/orsc.2020.1380.

80 *How will ESG performance shape your future? Climate Change and Sustainability Services (CCaSS) Fifth Institutional Investor Survey*, EYGM Limited, 2020. https://assets.ey.com/content/dam/ey-sites/ey-com/en_gl/topics/assurance/assurance-pdfs/ey-global-institutional-investor-survey-2020.pdf.

81 Detomasi, David A., "The Political Roots of Corporate Social Responsibility," *Journal of Business Ethics* 82, no. 4: 807–819, 26 October 2007. https://link.springer.com/article/10.1007/s10551-007-9594-y.

82 Bhanji, Zahra, and Joanne E. Oxley, "Overcoming the dual liability of foreign-ness and privateness in international corporate citizenship partnerships," *Journal of International Business Studies* 44, no. 4: 290–311, 11 April 2013. https://link.springer.com/article/10.1057/jibs.2013.8.

83 Oh, Chang H., Daniel Shapiro, Shuna S. H. Ho, and Jiyoung Shin, "Location matters: Valuing firm-specific nonmarket risk in the global mining industry," *Strategic Management Journal* 41, no. 7: 1210–1244, 26 March 2020. https://onlinelibrary.wiley.com/doi/full/10.1002/smj.3153.

84 *Geostrategy in Practice 2021*, EYGM Limited, 2021. https://www.ey.com/en_gl/geostrategy/the-ceo-imperative-are-you-making-political-risk-a-strategic-priority.

85 "Enterprise Risk Management: Integrating with Strategy and Performance," The Committee of Sponsoring Organizations (COSO). https://www.coso.org/guidance-erm.

86 Fraser, John R. S., and Betty J. Simkins, "The challenges of and solutions for implementing enterprise risk management," *Business Horizons* 59, no. 6: 689–698, 2016. http://dx.doi.org/10.1016/j.bushor.2016.06.007.

87 "What if the difference between adversity and advantage is a resilient board?" *EY Global Board Risk Survey 2023,* EYGM Limited, 2023. https://www.ey .com/en_gl/global-board-risk-survey/what-if-the-difference-between -adversity-and-advantage-is-a-resilient-board.

88 *What is Enterprise Risk Management?,* North Carolina State University, 2019. https://erm.ncsu.edu/az/erm/i/chan/library/What_is_ERM_July_2019.pdf.

89 Peterdy, Kyle, "PESTEL Analysis," Corporate Finance Institute, accessed 16 April 2024. https://corporatefinanceinstitute.com/resources/management /pestel-analysis/.

90 Frigo, Mark, Matteo Tonello, and Richard Anderson, "Strategic Risk Management: A Primer for Directors," Harvard Law School Forum on Corporate Governance, 23 August 2012. https://corpgov.law.harvard.edu/2012/08/23 /strategic-risk-management-a-primer-for-directors/.

91 *Geostrategy in Practice 2021,* EYGM Limited, 2021. https://assets.ey.com /content/dam/ey-sites/ey-com/en_gl/topics/geostrategy/ey-ceo-imperative -geostrategy-in-practice-2021.pdf.

92 "What if the difference between adversity and advantage is a resilient board?" *EY Global Board Risk Survey 2023,* EYGM Limited, 2023. https://www.ey.com /en_gl/global-board-risk-survey/what-if-the-difference-between-adversity -and-advantage-is-a-resilient-board.

93 "Fact Sheet: President Biden's Cap on the Cost of Insulin Could Benefit Millions of Americans in All 50 States," The White House Briefing Room, 02 March 2023. https://www.whitehouse.gov/briefing-room/statements -releases/2023/03/02/fact-sheet-president-bidens-cap-on-the-cost-of -insulin-could-benefit-millions-of-americans-in-all-50-states/.

94 "Lilly Cuts Insulin Prices by 70 Percent and Caps Patient Insulin Out-of-Pocket Costs at $35 Per Month," Eli Lilly and Company, 01 March 2023. https://investor .lilly.com/news-releases/news-release-details/lilly-cuts-insulin-prices-70-and -caps-patient-insulin-out-pocket.

95 *Geostrategy in Practice 2021,* EYGM Limited, 2021. https://assets.ey.com /content/dam/ey-sites/ey-com/en_gl/topics/geostrategy/ey-ceo-imperative -geostrategy-in-practice-2021.pdf.

96 *Geostrategy in Practice 2021,* EYGM Limited, 2021. https://assets.ey.com /content/dam/ey-sites/ey-com/en_gl/topics/geostrategy/ey-ceo-imperative -geostrategy-in-practice-2021.pdf.

97 Hollinger, Peggy, "Annual reports are fast becoming political treatises," *Financial Times,* 26 July 2023. https://on.ft.com/4534Qlc.

98 "Petroleo Brasileiro S.A. – Petrobas, Form 20-F," United States Securities and Exchange Commission, 31 December 2022. https://www.sec.gov/ix?doc=/Archives/edgar/data/0001119639/000129281423001253/pbrform20f_2022.htm.

99 "How to build a dynamic risk assessment," Ernst & Young LLP, 2021. https://www.ey.com/en_us/cro-risk/how-to-leverage-data-to-identify-emerging-risks.

100 *The CEO Imperative: How will CEOs respond to a new recession reality? EY CEO Outlook Pulse Survey - January 2023*, EYGM Limited, 2023. https://assets.ey.com/content/dam/ey-sites/ey-com/en_us/topics/ceo/ey-ceo-outlook-pulse-survey-january-2023-global-report.pdf.

101 *Geostrategy in Practice 2021*, EYGM Limited, 2021. https://assets.ey.com/content/dam/ey-sites/ey-com/en_gl/topics/geostrategy/ey-ceo-imperative-geostrategy-in-practice-2021.pdf.

102 *The CEO Imperative Series: How has adversity become the springboard to growth for CEOs? CEO Imperative Study 2021*, EYGM Limited, 2021. https://www.ey.com/en_gl/ceo/the-ceo-imperative-how-has-adversity-become-a-springboard-to-growth.

103 Preuss, Simone, "Will Ethiopia be the new Bangladesh?," Fashion United, 14 July 2015. https://fashionunited.com/news/fashion/will-ethiopia-be-the-new-bangladesh/201507147542.

104 Bavier, Joe, Anna Ringstrom, and Ruma Paul, "INSIGHT Ethiopia's war risks leaving manufacturing dreams in tatters," Reuters, 11 December 2020. https://www.reuters.com/world/asia-pacific/insight-ethiopias-war-risks-leaving-manufacturing-dreams-tatters-2020-12-11/.

105 Siegel, Nathan, "The Next Shirt You Buy May Say 'Made In Ethiopia.' Here's Why," NPR, 28 October 2014. https://www.npr.org/2014/10/28/359655632/the-next-shirt-you-buy-may-say-made-in-ethiopia-heres-why.

106 "Global Conflict Tracker: Conflict in Ethiopia," Council on Foreign Relations (CFR), updated 19 December 2023. https://www.cfr.org/global-conflict-tracker/conflict/conflict-ethiopia.

107 Lu, Sheng, "Should US Fashion Companies Continue to Diversify their Apparel Sourcing Bases in 2022?," *FASH455 Global Apparel & Textile Trade and Sourcing*, 15 March 2022. https://shenglufashion.com/2022/03/15/fash455-debate-should-us-fashion-companies-continue-to-diversify-their-apparel-sourcing-bases-in-2022/.

108 *Geostrategy in Practice 2021*, EYGM Limited, 2021. https://assets.ey.com/content/dam/ey-sites/ey-com/en_gl/topics/geostrategy/ey-ceo-imperative

-geostrategy-in-practice-2021.pdf.

109 *Geostrategy in Practice 2021*, EYGM Limited, 2021. https://assets.ey.com /content/dam/ey-sites/ey-com/en_gl/topics/geostrategy/ey-ceo-imperative -geostrategy-in-practice-2021.pdf.

110 "How will CEOs respond to a new recession reality?" *EY CEO Outlook Pulse Survey – January 2023*, EYGM Limited, 2023.

111 "If AI holds the answers, are CEOs asking the right strategic questions?" *EY CEO Outlook Pulse Survey – July 2023*, EYGM Limited, 2023.

112 *Geostrategy in Practice 2021*, EYGM Limited, 2021. https://assets.ey.com /content/dam/ey-sites/ey-com/en_gl/topics/geostrategy/ey-ceo-imperative -geostrategy-in-practice-2021.pdf.

113 *Will COVID-19 turbo-charge M&A and transformation? EY Global Capital Confidence Barometer February 2021*, EYGM Limited, 2021. https://assets.ey.com /content/dam/ey-sites/ey-com/en_gl/topics/ey-capital-confidence-barometer /ccb23/pdfs/ey-ccb23-mergers-acquisitions-strategy-study.pdf.

114 *Will COVID-19 turbo-charge M&A and transformation? EY Global Capital Confidence Barometer February 2021*, EYGM Limited, 2021. https://assets .ey.com/content/dam/ey-sites/ey-com/en_gl/topics/ey-capital-confidence -barometer/ccb23/pdfs/ey-ccb23-global-report-v02.pdf.

115 Mintzberg, Henry, "Patterns in Strategy Formation," *Management Science* 24, no. 9: 934–948, May 1978. https://www.jstor.org/stable/2630633.

116 Porter, Michael E., "What Is Strategy?," *Harvard Business Review*, November– December 1996. https://hbr.org/1996/11/what-is-strategy.

117 Oberholzer-Gee, Felix, *Better, Simpler Strategy: A Value-Based Guide to Exceptional Performance* (Boston, MA: Harvard Business Review Press, 2021). https://www.hbs.edu/faculty/Pages/item.aspx?num=59665.

118 *Geopolitical Risk and Disruption*, EYGM Limited and FCLT Global, 2022. https://www.fcltglobal.org/wp-content/uploads/Geopolitical-Risk-and -Disruption_-FCLTGlobal-EY.pdf.

119 *Geostrategy in Practice 2021*, EYGM Limited, 2021. https://assets.ey.com /content/dam/ey-sites/ey-com/en_gl/topics/geostrategy/ey-ceo-imperative -geostrategy-in-practice-2021.pdf.

120 *Socio-Economic Assessment Toolbox (S.E.A.T.)*, Anglo American plc, 2003. https://www.angloamerican.com/development/social/community -engagement/~/media/Files/A/Anglo-American-Plc/siteware/docs /seat_toolbox2.pdf.

121 Henisz, Witold, "How companies can successfully navigate political risks," Wharton School of the University of Pennsylvania, 8 June 2021. https://knowledge .wharton.upenn.edu/article/companies-can-successfully-navigate-political-risks/.

122 Jay, John, and Mervyn King, *Radical Uncertainty: decision-making beyond the numbers* (New York: W.W. Norton & Company, 2020). https://wwnorton .com/books/9781324004776.

123 *Geostrategy in Practice 2021*, EYGM Limited, 2021. https://assets.ey.com /content/dam/ey-sites/ey-com/en_gl/topics/geostrategy/ey-ceo-imperative -geostrategy-in-practice-2021.pdf.

124 Peattie, Ken, "Green Consumption: Behavior and Norms," *Annual Review of Environment and Resources* 35: 195–228, 12 August 2010. https://www .annualreviews.org/doi/pdf/10.1146/annurev-environ-032609-094328.

125 *Unilever Environmental Performance Report 2000*, Unilever plc, 2000. https:// www.unilever.com/files/origin/c0b606f348d59c5f65e3fd718a0c3bb13a6da020 .pdf/2000-unilever-environmental-performance-how-we-care-for-the -environment.pdf.

126 *Unilever Sustainable Living Plan 2010–2020: Summary of 10 Years' Progress*, Unilever plc, 2021. https://www.unilever.com/files/92ui5egz /production/16cb778e4d31b81509dc5937001559f1f5c863ab.pdf.

127 *Unilever Sustainable Living Plan 2010–2020: Summary of 10 Years' Progress*, Unilever plc, 2021. https://www.unilever.com/files/92ui5egz /production/16cb778e4d31b81509dc5937001559f1f5c863ab.pdf.

128 "Sustainability reporting centre: Reporting Archive," Unilever. https:// www.unilever.com/planet-and-society/sustainability-reporting-centre /reporting-archive/.

129 "Sustainability Governance," Unilever. https://www.unilever .com/planet-and-society/sustainability-reporting-centre /our-sustainability-governance/.

130 "Brands with purpose grow – and here's the proof," Unilever plc, 11 June 2019. https://www.unilever.com/news/news-search/2019 /brands-with-purpose-grow-and-here-is-the-proof/.

131 "Unilever's purpose-led brands outperform," Unilever plc, 11 June 2019. https://www.unilever.com/news/press-and-media/press-releases/2019 /unilevers-purpose-led-brands-outperform/.

132 "Unilever's purpose-led brands outperform," Unilever plc, 11 June 2019. https://www.unilever.com/news/press-and-media/press-releases/2019 /unilevers-purpose-led-brands-outperform/.

133 "Unilever celebrates 10 years of the Sustainable Living Plan," Unilever plc, 06 May 2020. https://www.unilever.com/news/press-and-media/press -releases/2020/unilever-celebrates-10-years-of-the-sustainable-living-plan/.

134 "Profit through purpose: Eight years of pioneering and learning," Unilever plc, 12 April 2019. https://www.unilever.com/news/news-search/2019 /profit-through-purpose-eight-years-of-pioneering-and-learning/.

135 *Unilever's supply chain*, Unilever plc, 2023. https://www.unilever.com /files/8c652127-8ea5-4db0-bedb-f03a37637285/supply-chain-overview -spend-analysis---may-2022--1-.pdfly%20chain%20disruptions%20and%20 resource%20price%20volatility.

136 O'Donnell, Grace, "Sustainability 'contributes to the bottom line,' Unilever CEO says," *Yahoo! News*, 05 November 2022. https://news.yahoo.com /sustainability-bottom-line-unilever-122328043.html.

137 *2023 Weinreb Group Chief Sustainability Officer Report*, Weinreb Group, 2023. https://weinrebgroup.com/wp-content/uploads/2023/03/2023-CSO-Report.pdf.

138 *C-suite Insights: Sustainability and ESG Trends Index*, EYGM Limited, 2023. https://www.ey.com/en_us/sustainability/sustainability-and-esg-trends-index.

139 *The Chief Sustainability Officer, 10 Years Later*, Weinreb Group, 2021. https://weinrebgroup.com/wp-content/uploads/2021/05/Weinreb-Group -Sustainability-and-ESG-Recruiting-The-Chief-Sustainability-Officer-10 -years-Later-The-Rise-of-ESG-in-the-C-Suite-2021-Report.pdf.

140 *Geostrategy in Practice 2021*, EYGM Limited, 2021. https://assets.ey.com /content/dam/ey-sites/ey-com/en_gl/topics/geostrategy/ey-ceo-imperative -geostrategy-in-practice-2021.pdf.

141 *EY Geostrategy in Practice 2021*, EYGM Limited, 2021. https://assets.ey.com /content/dam/ey-sites/ey-com/en_gl/topics/geostrategy/ey-ceo-imperative -geostrategy-in-practice-2021.pdf.

142 *Geostrategy in Practice 2021*, EYGM Limited, 2021. https://assets.ey.com /content/dam/ey-sites/ey-com/en_gl/topics/geostrategy/ey-ceo-imperative -geostrategy-in-practice-2021.pdf.

143 *Geostrategy in Practice 2021*, EYGM Limited, 2021. https://assets.ey.com /content/dam/ey-sites/ey-com/en_gl/topics/geostrategy/ey-ceo-imperative -geostrategy-in-practice-2021.pdf.

144 *Geostrategy in Practice 2021*, EYGM Limited, 2021. https://assets.ey.com /content/dam/ey-sites/ey-com/en_gl/topics/geostrategy/ey-ceo-imperative -geostrategy-in-practice-2021.pdf.

145 *Geostrategy in Practice 2021*, EYGM Limited, 2021. https://assets.ey.com /content/dam/ey-sites/ey-com/en_gl/topics/geostrategy/ey-ceo-imperative -geostrategy-in-practice-2021.pdf.

146 *Geopolitical Risk and Disruption: A Conversation Guide for Management and Board Directors*, EYGM Limited and FCLT Global, 2022. https://www.fcltglobal.org /resource/geopolitical-risk-ey/.

147 *Geostrategy in Practice 2021*, EYGM Limited, 2021. https://assets.ey.com /content/dam/ey-sites/ey-com/en_gl/topics/geostrategy/ey-ceo-imperative -geostrategy-in-practice-2021.pdf.

148 *How can boards prioritize resilience to build trust and create value? EY Global Board Risk Survey 2023*, EYGM Limited, 2023. https://assets.ey.com/content /dam/ey-sites/ey-com/en_gl/topics/global-board-risk-survey/ey-global -board-risk-survey-2023.pdf.

149 *Geostrategy in Practice 2021*, EYGM Limited, 2021. https://assets.ey.com /content/dam/ey-sites/ey-com/en_gl/topics/geostrategy/ey-ceo-imperative -geostrategy-in-practice-2021.pdf.

150 *How can boards prioritize resilience to build trust and create value? EY Global Board Risk Survey 2023*, EYGM Limited, 2023. https://assets.ey.com/content /dam/ey-sites/ey-com/en_gl/topics/global-board-risk-survey/ey-global -board-risk-survey-2023.pdf.

151 *Geostrategy in Practice 2021*, EYGM Limited, 2021. https://assets.ey.com /content/dam/ey-sites/ey-com/en_gl/topics/geostrategy/ey-ceo-imperative -geostrategy-in-practice-2021.pdf.

ABOUT THE AUTHORS

Courtney Rickert McCaffrey is the EY Global Insights Leader for the EY Geostrategic Business Group. She is a recognized thought leader in political risk, global macro trends, and methodologies such as risk indices, scenario analysis, and horizon scanning. She has previously worked at Kearney, Eurasia Group, and the US International Development Finance Corporation. Courtney earned her BA from Drake University and her MA from the Johns Hopkins School of Advanced International Studies.

Witold J. Henisz is the Vice Dean and Faculty Director of the ESG Initiative and Deloitte & Touche Professor of Management at the Wharton School, The University of Pennsylvania. His research examines the impact of political hazards as well as environmental, social, and governance factors more broadly on the strategy and valuation of global corporations. He received his PhD from University of California, Berkeley, and previously received an MA in international relations from the Johns Hopkins School of Advanced International Studies.

Oliver Jones is the EY Global Markets and Sustainability Leader for Strategy and Transactions (SaT) services. He also leads the experienced global geopolitical advisory team, the EY Geostrategic Business Group, which assists clients in understanding the business implications of the ongoing geopolitical disruption in the world today. Prior to starting his career in consulting, he was a senior civil servant in the UK government. He earned an MA in geography from the University of Cambridge.

EY | Building a better working world

EY exists to build a better working world, helping to create long-term value for clients, people and society and build trust in the capital markets.

Enabled by data and technology, diverse EY teams in over 150 countries provide trust through assurance and help clients grow, transform and operate.

Working across assurance, consulting, law, strategy, tax and transactions, EY teams ask better questions to find new answers for the complex issues facing our world today.

EY refers to the global organization, and may refer to one or more, of the member firms of Ernst & Young Global Limited, each of which is a separate legal entity. Ernst & Young Global Limited, a UK company limited by guarantee, does not provide services to clients. Information about how EY collects and uses personal data and a description of the rights individuals have under data protection legislation are available via ey.com/privacy. EY member firms do not practice law where prohibited by local laws. For more information about our organization, please visit ey.com.

ABOUT EY-PARTHENON

EY-Parthenon teams work with clients to navigate complexity by helping them to reimagine their ecosystems, reshape their portfolios and reinvent themselves for a better future. With global connectivity and scale, EY-Parthenon teams focus on Strategy Realized — helping CEOs design and deliver strategies to better manage challenges while maximizing opportunities as they look to transform their businesses. From idea to implementation, EY-Parthenon teams help organizations to build a better working world by fostering long-term value. EY-Parthenon is a brand under which a number of EY member firms across the globe provide strategy consulting services. For more information, please visit ey.com/parthenon.